Book 3 from the Relationsh[...]
Seminar Series, *"The Teacher Down the Hall"*

I'm Listening!

Highly Effective Communication
is *not* measured by how much you *Say*,
but in how well you *Listen*.

By
TOD FALLER

"I'm Listening!"

By

Tod Faller

copyright ©2007 Tod Faller

All rights reserved. No part of this publication may be reproduced or transmitted in any other form or for any means, electronic or mechanical, including photocopy, recording or any information storage system, without written permission from Headline Books, Inc.

**To order additional copies of this book or
for book publishing information, or to contact the author:**

Headline Books, Inc.
P.O. Box 52
Terra Alta, WV 26764
www.headlinebooks.com

Tel/Fax: 800-570-595
Email: tod@todfaller.com
www.todfaller.com

ISBN 0-929915-70-4
ISBN-13: 978-0-929915-70-8

Library of Congress Control Number: 2007931930

PRINTED IN THE UNITED STATES OF AMERICA

Dedication

*To my son Scott and his wife, my daughter in-law,
for teaching incredible Life Lessons.
You have proven that we are never too old to be Learners...
even if nobody else understands the Lessons.*

...and, as always, for our grandbabies:

Emily—Aaron—Andrew

We have always loved you.

Table of Contents

Foreword 5

Introduction 8

Section I Communication Basics:

Chapter 1 UNDERSTANDING: The Insatiable Quest 13

Chapter 2 COMMUNICATION:
The Union between Attitude and Understanding 17

Chapter 3 RUMORS: The Absence of Understanding 25

Chapter 4 INTRAPERSONAL BEHAVIORS: Establishing the *NEED* to Listen 29

Section II Obstacles to Listening:

Chapter 5 OBSTACLES TO LISTENING: "It's all about ME" 39

Chapter 6 OBSTACLES TO LISTENING: ONE ON ONE 43

Chapter 7 OBSTACLES TO LISTENING: IN GROUPS 47

Section III Are You Listening?

Chapter 8 HEARING IS NOT LISTENING! 65

Chapter 9 WORDS: Watts in a Word? 67

Chapter 10 INFLECTION:
MORE important Than the Truth of Your Message 77

Chapter 11 BODY LANGUAGE AND OTHER NON-VERBALS:
What you're saying when you're saying NOTHING at all! 80

Chapter 12 PUTTING IT ALL TOGETHER:
From PASSIVE to ACTIVE...in 21 Days...Guaranteed! 92

Epilogue 106

Foreword

"The Teacher Down the Hall" Seminar Series

ONCE UPON A TIME, there was a young school teacher who had a gift for entering the world of children. She understood that all people have different experiences. She knew that children might want similar things, but that they will choose different behaviors to get what they want. She did not assume that people were acting in an unnatural way merely because their choices in behaviors differed from her own.

She had just moved into the area and had accepted a position in a nearby school district to teach in a rural elementary school. She would become the sixth teacher in this particular fifth grade class classroom *this year*—and it was only January. At the time, of course, she wasn't aware that so many teachers had already been assigned to this class... and had within weeks, walked out.

The other teachers in the building saw so many other teachers come and go before her, they didn't even bother to learn her name. They were so sure that she, too, would not last, they referred to her only as **The TEACHER DOWN the HALL.** (Her story is in book two: *"So THAT'S why you're like that!"*)

This Seminar Series was inspired by a very real West Virginia school teacher in a very real West Virginia rural elementary school. This teacher not only stayed for the rest of the year, she went on to become an award winning teacher *and* school principal. In fact, to this day, her former students still seek her out. They will find her at the grocery store, at the mall, or knock on the front door of her house. They will bring their children to introduce them to the person they still call **THE** Teacher. They want to know if she will *"Talk to my kids, like you talked to me."* And they ask her if she will *"Teach me to LISTEN to my kids, like you listened to us."*

When I wrote for higher education, I was expected to write *TO the knowledge* (to expound upon the knowledge*), as opposed to writing *FOR the understanding* of the reader. When I was encouraged to make this seminar series available as individual books, my intent was to write so that the knowledge could be easily *"understood and applied."* My objective was to write for pre-teens and teenagers... *and* their parents and teachers...a layman's guide through those turbulent times from middle school through high school. My hope was to promote understanding of our human Behaviors and Needs while providing practical strategies that could be used to build and sustain positive relationships.

Each book, as each seminar in the series, was written to be another step in the process of helping teens… *and* parents, families, students, teachers, coworkers, and employers… to *UNDERSTAND, ACCEPT, and RESOLVE* their Interpersonal Conflicts. These books are, I understand, being used to train Peer Tutors in Character Education and Responsible Student Education programs, in Relationship Building Seminars, and in teacher "book study" groups to help staffs build stronger rapport within their school communities.

The first book in the series is *"What did you do THAT for?"* The second was *"So THAT'S why you're like that."* You are about to enter the third book in the series, *"I'm LISTENING!"* A fourth book, a companion reader of motivational stories taken from the series, is called: *LESSONS for LEADERS*.

After hundreds of presentations of these seminars, to thousands of participants in schools and business across the country, the goals remain the same:
- To instill understanding
- To encourage acceptance
- To establish open communication and sustained relationships
- To diminish Intrapersonal confusion and resolve Interpersonal conflicts

UNDERSTANDING: Our behaviors are our actions and are as numerous as the stars in the sky. Our basic human Needs, however, can be counted on the fingers of one hand. The drive to meet our basic human Needs is the motivation behind every behavior.

All behaviors are simply each person's best attempts to meet his/her basic human Needs. Our behaviors give the appearance that we are so different. *Conflict* begins when someone tells us "NO." Behaviors to *Control* begin when we won't take "NO" for an answer. The seeds of Conflict are <u>planted</u> when we first fail to look beyond the behavior we find disagreeable or inappropriate to recognize the Need that motivated that behavior. Without such an understanding, we remain suspicious and defensive of others; we say others are wrong, misguided, or sinister if they don't behave the way we think they *should* behave. How many of us, out of sheer frustration, have shouted, *"What did you do THAT for?"*

ACCEPTANCE: The seeds of discontent and conflict <u>take root</u> when we refuse to *accept* that ALL humans have the right to make creative, responsible, and independent choices for themselves. Intellectually, we know that that we can't control what others say or do, but somehow, we feel compelled to try. The more we persist in "getting our way" or the longer we resist accepting unwelcome behaviors from those we don't understand or cannot otherwise control—the higher the walls we build between us. If I can understand the root of your behaviors, I can grow to separate YOU from your behaviors. The gift we offer each other is not in *understanding* that we're different…the gift we offer is in *accepting* that we're different.

RESOLUTION: The path to *resolving* conflict is in accepting this simple premise: *People fail to see others as they are… only as they want them to be.* Herein lies the conflict… or the reduction and resolution of conflict. Determined by the path you choose, conflict will flourish…or wither and die on the vine. The reduction and resolution of conflict in your life is dependent upon your ability and *willingness* to look beyond the negative, nonproductive, or inappropriate behaviors of others.

The key to Conflict Resolution, therefore, is to look *past* the behaviors we don't like or understand in others, to discover the Need that is driving that behavior. There are endless behaviors "out there," but there are only five (5) basic human Needs. People can't always have everything they want, but they always get some of what they Need. If you are willing to look beyond the behavior, to serve the Need *others* are trying to meet, you will be amazed to find that others will go out of their way to meet *your* Needs, and they won't even realize why they're doing it… guaranteed!

Introduction

"I'm Listening!"

"Listening is LOVE in action."
—Scott Peck, *The Road Less Traveled*

This seminar series has been developed to help participants and readers meet their basic human Needs. This third book in the series is directed primarily to meeting your **Need to be Affirmed**. This is your Need to be patted on the back, fulfilled, recognized with a sense of importance, to be taken seriously, to be really understood and to be truly *listened* to. This is one of the (five) basic Human Needs that *all* of us have in common.

Eli and his student Samuel had chosen to rest from their travels and to spend the night in the temple. Eli was in one of the anti-rooms and Samuel in another. As Samuel prepared to lie down for the night he heard his name being called. Samuel got up and walked to Eli and said, *"Yes, master, you called?"*
"No," replied the master, *"I did not call you Samuel, go to sleep."*
Having returned to his chamber, Samuel again prepared for sleep, when for a second time, he heard someone call his name. Obediently, he got up and walked back to Eli and said, *"Yes, master, you called?"*
Once again, the patient master said, *"No, I did not call; go back to sleep."*
For a third time, Samuel prepared for sleep. Yet, once again, he heard the call for *"Samuel."* And once again, he walked to Eli and said, *"You called, master?"*
Finally, Eli understood. *"It is not I who calls your name, Samuel,"* he began. *"Go back now, and this time when you hear your name, say 'Speak, Lord, your servant is listening.'"*

Listening is something we **learn**. It takes a sincere and conscious effort. Many people believe they are good listeners merely because they have ears; the capacity to hear. As I sit here, I can hear the creaking of the floor, the birds outside the window and the sound of bacon frying in the pan. This requires no real effort on my part. I "listen" whenever such momentary distractions pull my brain from its current cycle of thought back to awareness, to register *sound* and its *significance* to me. As Eli was trying to teach Samuel, hearing when others speak goes way beyond the words people say… it is listening with your ***whole heart, your whole mind…and your whole spirit.***

Father Powell...that's Father John Powell, PhD...priest, author, and an exceptional public speaker, has written a dozen or more books on Interpersonal Communications. As with a generation of psychologist and psychotherapist who have preceded him, he recognized the basic human **Need to be Affirmed**. *"You cannot over emphasize the immense Need all humans have to be taken seriously, to be really understood, and to be truly **listened** to."*

It is not an emotional fancy. Each of us has the inherent human Need *to be heard* and *really* understood. *"I'm Listening!"* is my invitation to you to gain a better understanding as to why most of us can hear, but few of us listen. It's an invitation to understand how you can get what you want. It is an invitation to realize how *you can be taken seriously, be really understood and be truly listened to.* If you want a closer relationship with those with whom you work and live, this can happen through a better understanding of how we humans communicate; how we read and interpret our Words, Inflection, and Body Language.

Your ability to build rapport and to communicate with others is absolutely *dependent* upon your use of these three basic communications tools: *Words, Inflection, and Body Language.* If your goal is to better understand others, and if you are willing for others to better understand you, then you will enjoy and benefit from reading: *"I'm Listening!"* To communicate...to develop a *common-union* with others...it is essential to understand what we say, from what we *intended* to say; how we say it...or don't say it; and what we convey...or meant to convey when we said it.

Words are nothing more than labels for our experiences; the unseen pictures in the mind. Inflection assigns texture… both feeling and perspective to those pictures. Body language brings those mental pictures to life… exposing that which has remained unspoken. The intent of this book is to help you leap from a world where you have been conditioned to *hearing* only with your ears to accepting that there is an entire world of listening through observation and conscious awareness. Your ability to build rapport with others is dependent upon your willingness and ability to do so.

This world of *listening* through observation, you will find, may be an entire universe beyond the world to which you may have been accustomed. The most amazing part is… you will find others *Listening* to *You*. They will do it willingly…they will do it for life…and they won't even know why they're doing it… guaranteed!

SECTION I of this book is intended to **establish the foundation for listening**. Sherlock Holmes often said, *"People see but they do not observe."* In the same regard, it can be said that *"People hear but they do not listen."* Hearing and Listening are about as closely related as lightning would be to the lightning bug. Our choices to seek personal happiness and positive relationships are dependent upon not just our ability to *hear* but in our willingness to *understand* what we hear, i.e., *to listen* to each other.

SECTION II asks the question; **Are *you* listening?** Fifty percent of verbal communication requires that we not only speak, but that we also listen. Experience has taught me that before individuals are ready to learn the relationship building skills of Active Listening, people first appreciate hearing some of the obstacles to listening: why people can't, don't, won't, or haven't been listening. Learn how the dynamics of the classroom and large group settings, your one-on-one conversations, and the composition of the brain hinders your relationships. In a seminar setting, it is still fun watching people as they come to the realization, after oh so many years, that listening and hearing are not synonymous terms. It is like lifting a veil.

SECTION III gets at the heart of **highly effective communications** and more positive relationship building skills. Throughout this section you will be provided with tangible strategies for Active Listening, building relationships and resolving conflict. You will do this by understanding and utilizing the ways that all people use to accept and communicate with each other: through our words, our inflections, our body language, and other non-verbal expressions.

It will be through this awareness…how to read, utilize and integrate the words, inflection and body language…that *Active* Listening becomes possible. To be truly listened to is a basic human Need. Work to meet this Need in others, and you will immediately discover others going out of their way to meet YOUR Needs…Guaranteed!

I would tell you to sit back and enjoy this third book in the series…but the operative word in Active Listening…is to be *ACTIVE*. You will be asked to actively participate…to become involved… to practice these skills. If you really do want a better relationship with your son or daughter, your spouse, your students, or the teacher down the hall, before you walk away from this book, I will ask you to accept the 21 Day Challenge. If you are willing to follow through on that challenge, incorporating the skills and understanding provided, you will discover how others will treat you differently…more positively…and go out of their way to meet YOUR Needs. All this because your words, inflection and body language are now saying, *"I'm Listening!"*

Section I

Communication Basics:

In the absence of fact, in the void between reality and speculation, we are so hungry to be "in the know" that we will create our own understanding. We will seek counsel from other people who also admit they don't know...and we call this Communications.

Chapters

    1. UNDERSTANDING: Man's (Woman's) Insatiable Quest

    2. COMMUNICATIONS: The Union between Attitude and Understanding

    3. RUMORS: The Absence of Understanding

    4. INTRAPERSONAL BEHAVIORS: Establishing the NEED to Listen

Chapter 1

Understanding: The Insatiable Quest

"How will I know if what you said is really what you meant?"

Louie, a foreign exchange student, was enrolled in an English speaking class. At the end of the class, Louie was asked to show his understanding of the lesson by putting the new words he learned into a sentence. The words were Pink, Green, and Yellow. Louie thought for a moment before proudly proclaiming: *"When de phone goes GREEN, GREEN, GREEN, I PINK it up and say YELLOW!"*

It is said that if you want to be understood, you must first be willing to understand. You must be willing to understand what *others* are really saying to you, and you must understand what messages *you* are sending to them. There are three ways, and only three ways, we humans have to understand each other: Through our Words, Inflection, and Body Language.

Understanding is vital. This is the holy grail for humans: the quest for understanding. If you don't understand, you speculate; when you speculate, you're guessing; when you're guessing, you still don't know; if you don't know, you don't understand. When you are seeking understanding in this manner you are just *thinking* about what it is you don't know…but *want* to know. You're so anxious to understand what you don't know, you actually ask *other* people who also admit they don't know. Satisfied only in the knowledge that you are not alone in the darkness, you exhaust yourself thinking more about what you (and others) readily admit you still don't understand.

In the absence of fact, in the void between reality and speculation, we are so hungry to be *"in the know"* that we will *create* our own understanding…our own truth. The longer we just think about what it is we don't understand, the easier it becomes to *imagine* what the truth *must be*. We substitute imagination for communications and allow *this* to become our understanding.

We keep hearing, for example, about the Loch Ness Monster. He (She? It?) has been peaking the curiosity of man forever. Dozens of attempts to understand and to discover "the truth," however, have failed to reveal evidence of "Nessie." We just don't know what lies beneath the water of the Loch. Perhaps there is no monster and that is the truth. But our human nature demands to know *for sure.* In the absence of absolute evidence, each of us will have to believe what our imagination tells us is out there. That won't substitute for really understanding what's down there, of course, but we must allow ourselves to believe *something* while we wait for the facts. As a result, the "truth" becomes whatever YOU want it to be.

We watch magicians make tigers appear in an empty cage; we are amazed to see airplanes disappear in front of our eyes; and we hold our breath each time the pretty lady gets sawed in half. We want to know, *How did he do that?* Everyone has a theory. Everyone wants to understand.

In recent years, the "Masked Magician" has been doing his best to reveal how these illusions are being performed. He has succeeded in taking the mystery out of some of the magic tricks that have been keeping audiences on the edges of their seats forever. Consequently, we no longer have to speculate how the lady gets sawed in half. We now know the trick. Now that we really do understand, we don't have to guess anymore. In fact, when we truly understand, our appetite "to know" is appeased and our need for further speculation, i.e., guessing, rumors, gossip, about what we didn't understand, simply vanishes.

Our need to understand each other and to effectively communicate with our environment has been a quest men and women have been chasing forever, since the prophets to the present. From earliest times, natives used drums, Indians used smoke, sailors used lights, and Morris used his code. All through our history, we dedicate our day...every day...trying to communicate with other people, animals, and other living things in our environment.

How about our ability to "communicate" with animals? We give our pets human names, provide them the same creature comforts that we demand for ourselves; they sleep with us, we make over them, they love us back, we treat them like family (or better than family) and we often say, *"My dog thinks he's human."* How many of us talk to our dogs? Certainly they can't talk, so why do we think our pets can understand?

My wife sends the puppy outside, tail between his legs, as he shows the appropriate signs of remorse for chewing on her new slippers. While the words used to correct the pup may not have been completely understood by the little fella, I'm sure he understood my wife's tone, her body language... her message. The dog's body language corresponded fittingly to the elevation in my wife's inflection and rapid movements to communicate her displeasure...at his pleasure.

My sister "talks" to her cats. She says they understand her and come when they're called. She explains this to me as she waves a bowl of cat treats in front of them to coincide with her verbal calling of *"Kitty, Kitty, Kitty."* True, they will come to her...and only her. They obviously are "listening" to her and not to me. Assuming they can't speak or understand English, it is, nonetheless, obvious that they are clearly able to distinguish her presence from mine. They seem to be *reading* the lilt of her voice, her tone, her compassion, her motions and mannerisms. Her familiarity with them 'tells' those cats that they are loved and need not feel threatened by her. Me, they are not sure of, certainly don't listen to, and obviously don't care whether I am offended by their air of indifference or not. (While cats are not people, they certainly *act* like people.)

Have you ever heard of Koco the Gorilla? Koco's handler was Dr. Penny Patterson. Dr. Patterson's thesis was to prove that she could communicate with another living, albeit nonhuman, creature. The problem was how to "talk" with an animal that could not use speech to communicate. Koco, therefore, from a very early age, was taught sign language as a way by which Penny and Koco could develop a common understanding. Now, over 30 years old and as opinionated as any adult human, Koco speaks… through signing… more than 600 words and phrases to openly proclaim his wants, needs, fears, loves and hopes. Koco and Penny understand each other and have formed a common-union. If they can now "communicate," does this make Koco human?

Man has even been able to understand the creatures in the sea. In Florida, in cooperation with the U.S. Navy, since prior to World War II, marvelous and surprising experiments have been conducted to communicate with dolphins. While communicating with clicks, whistles, and sign language, these graceful and highly intelligent creatures have worked in cooperation with man to do much more than *speak* to us. Today these ocean dwellers are being employed to perform dozens of tasks in support of their human cousins: detecting shipping, scanning and mapping oceans, aiding in open sea and underwater rescue, and even cooperating with humans as part of an anti-terrorism harbor patrol task force.

We humans were able to read and understand the weather long before "Doppler" came on the scene. Our parents and grandparents taught us to forecast the weather. They understood how to watch the morning and evening sky and recite the rhyme: *"Red sky at night, sailors delight: Red sky in the morning, sailors take warning."* We can read the signs and sense the change in seasons. The seasons give way when the buds push out of the soil, when the leaves begin to change, and when the sun lowers in the southern sky. My grandmother knew when it was going to rain, she would say, because her *"bones would ache."* Even though these are less than scientific methods, we have been taught how to *understand* the world around us.

In the same way that we want to read, interpret and understand our environment and other living creatures, we make every effort also to read, interpret and understand the mood of the nation. The mere mention of certain "trigger" words or phrases, such as *abortion, gay marriage, 9/11, discrimination, or Katrina*, can instantly draw mental images and ignite emotions. Mental assessments, judgments, social agendas, political firestorms, and pictures of how life "should be" follow such charged statements. When we stand on opposite sides of emotional issues, this absence of common ground translates into the absence of communications.

Do you remember your first date? Remember how nervous you were? You said you weren't nervous, of course, but your body language probably gave you away. Maybe you shifted nervously from foot to foot, you fumbled with your change, you didn't know what to do with your hands, or you searched aimlessly for words as the conversation lagged. As a result, your body language was communicating something entirely different from your words. You said you weren't nervous, but your words and your actions did not connect. You left your date guessing, trying to *understand* what lay beyond the mask you were wearing. And when you told her one thing, and the message did not connect, she was left wondering… trying to understand your actions from your intentions; the message received from the message you hoped to convey. Communication, i.e., understanding, is never in the *intent* of the speaker, only in the message *received* by the listener.

A Final Thought:

We can, to some degree, understand plants and animals and we can discern the mood of a nation and even understand the weather. So why is it so difficult for us to understand each other? If understanding is every human's quest, how far along on this quest are you? Are you ready to learn how to "read" or better understand people? More importantly, are you ready for others to better read and better understand YOU?

Chapter 2

Communication: The Union between Attitude and Understanding

Communication is never in the intent of the speaker; communication is always in the message received by the listener.

As the new mall was being built, thousands of motorists could watch its progress as they traveled the nearby interstate. One morning, on the way past, we could see painters setting their scaffolds. The structure had already had been painted, so it was clear that the paint crews would now be painting a contrasting, horizontal color, three blocks high all the way around the building. One crew set up on the far right corner of the huge, multilevel building, while another crew set up on the far left side of the building.

That evening, we could see the freshly painted line was complete. Around the entire structure, our new mall now supported, for the whole world to see, a bright red line, two feet high, brilliantly accenting the white building. Two crews...one assignment. Unfortunately, in the absence of communications, each crew started on a different level. When they came around the corner, the line did not connect. As the building came into view, my wife Irene, who was sitting beside me, saw it first. Her immediate response summed it up nicely: *"Gentlemen, it would appear that what we have here is a failure to communicate."*

A *common union* is something that connects two like substances.
True Communication is evident in the link... the common-union... that emotionally connects two (or more) entities (plants, animals or people). Similar to the visual accent line(s) now adorning the new mall, when you and I fail to connect emotionally with others, we claim that either a lack of understanding or a lack of willingness to cooperate is to blame. And, of course, we're sure that the problem in making that connection would be the *other* guy's fault.

Relationships form in the delicate balance between an *understanding* of our five

(5) basic human Needs (to be Loved and Accepted; Affirmed and Fulfilled; Fun; Freedom; Survival) and how willing we are at *accepting* the behaviors other choose to meet those Needs. How willing are you to accept the behaviors of others if they differ from what *you* would do? Our very existence is dependent upon the lines of communication that we form with others. True communication is when *understanding* unites with a willing *attitude* to form a relationship; to form a common-union.

True communications is what happens when you and I, in our naturally persistent efforts to meet our wants and Needs, find harmony. To meet your wants and Needs, therefore, it requires the cooperation with *someone else* to make that happen. Unless you prefer to live as a hermit on a deserted island, you *need* other people to help you get what you want. Which means, each of us *needs the other* to get our Human Needs met.

To get what *you* want, you must convey your wishes and acknowledge that your expectations have (or have not) been met. To do that, you will choose *Behaviors* (to include *Controlling* Behaviors) that *you* believe will get you what you want. You will express them openly and honestly, or you will attempt to act out what you are thinking. To increase your chances of success, you will make your best attempt to *communicate*...to form a *common-union* with others. You will base each new attempt (behavior) on the *Feedback* you received from your past *Experiences*. You will work to build a relationship where the Wants and Needs of both can be mutually Understood, Accepted, and Resolved.

Note: This is the cycle of behavior all humans follow: a path we will trace more than 50,000 times a day.

The Behavior Cycle:

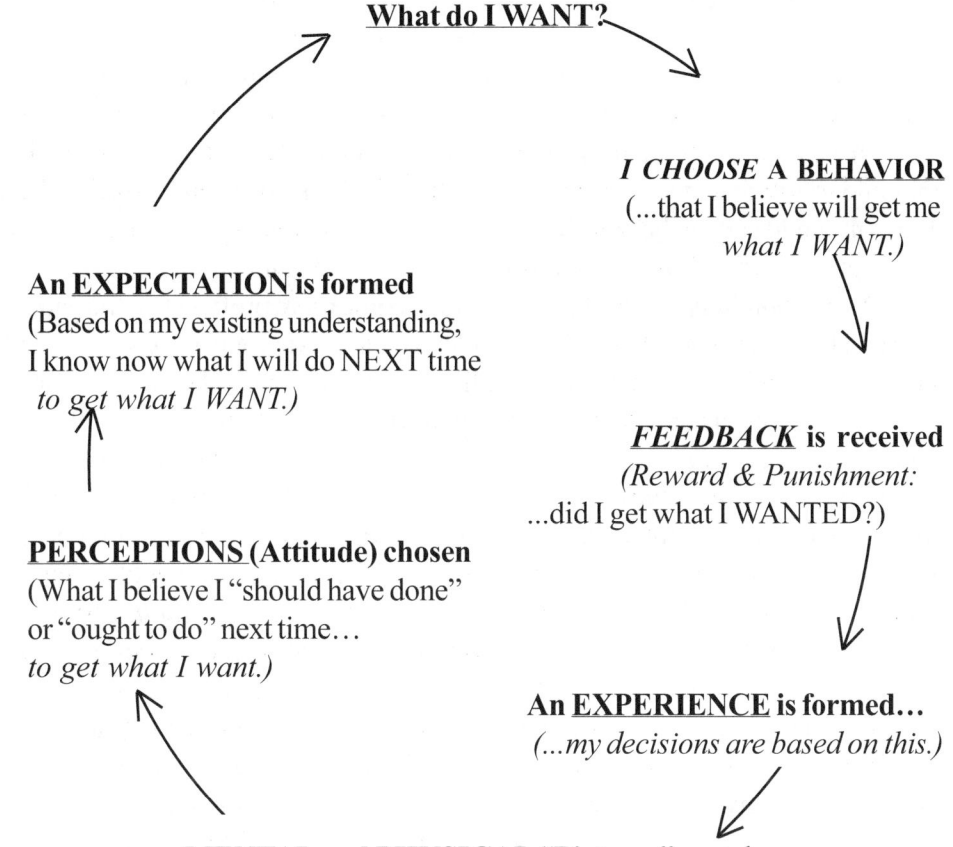

What do I WANT?

***I CHOOSE* A BEHAVIOR**
(...that I believe will get me
what I WANT.)

***FEEDBACK* is received**
(*Reward & Punishment:*
...did I get what I WANTED?)

An EXPERIENCE is formed...
(*...my decisions are based on this.*)

MENTAL and PHYSICAL "Pictures" are taken
(*"Snapshots" of the Experience are filed away*
for future reference and immediate recall.)

PERCEPTIONS (Attitude) chosen
(What I believe I "should have done"
or "ought to do" next time…
to get what I want.)

An EXPECTATION is formed
(Based on my existing understanding,
I know now what I will do NEXT time
to get what I WANT.)

All Behaviors are learned —All Behaviors are choices —All Behaviors can change. Behaviors will change; the CYCLE by which we choose our Behaviors, however, will NOT change.

When playing a game of "Catch" with your child, the ball must be passed back and forth to experience success. To keep the ball in play is the nature and purpose of the game of "Catch." Communications is much like playing ball: the nature and purpose of communications is to keep "the ball" in play.

When your child was just an infant, he (she) sat (or was propped up against the couch), and you slowly rolled the ball to him. You and the child would spread your legs out wide in order to ensure success by making sure the child "caught" the ball. As time went on, and the child got a bit older, the ball could be rolled a little faster, and his ability to roll it back would be more controlled and accurate as it came back to you. When the child could coordinate his hands to actually hold and catch the ball, you didn't need to roll it anymore. You tossed it in a slow, underhand way. You made sure the child was prepared for the ball, saying, "Ready?" and then gently making the toss. When the child caught the ball, you praised the child, clapped your hands, and invited other adults to watch how splendidly the child "played ball."

As the months pass, the child grows to become more proficient in the game. She (he) had learned to catch the ball more often and to better control the accuracy of the throw. You could throw overhand, but still not too hard. A natural trust was established and with it, an understanding that neither would throw the ball more forcefully than the other was prepared to receive it. If one occasionally dropped the ball, it was deemed an acceptable action as the occasional mistake or periods of inattention were viewed as unintentional. A dropped ball was not grounds for either party to suddenly stop playing the game and stomp away. In the same way, neither party would anticipate the other to simply toss the ball in another direction and say, *"go get it."* And neither party expected the other to suddenly feel compelled to begin pitching the ball directly at the other's head! We only do that in the *absence* of communications.

Communications is *exactly* like this. To establish a relationship with another, you must first take a chance...and start by "rolling the ball" in his/her direction. The ball, of course, is the conversation that starts off with generic, safe, innocuous comments or questions such as, *"Nice day we're having, isn't it?" "Think it will rain?"* or, *"Hello, how are you?"* Like rolling the ball, this is a safe way to introduce the "ball" into play. These are non-threatening and therefore, safe comments. No one will get hurt with such an opening pitch. You know the ball won't get away from you so you need not fear that you will be judged. I won't have to reveal anything about myself or be held accountable for some unknown fault in such a non-threatening exchange.

As in any game of catch, as trust is formed, both players become more comfortable with the game. Both feel more confident in risking the occasional comment that might mean the other would have to stretch a little or 0jump to catch the ball. The unspoken understanding is, *"you will not be judged for your occasional poor throws."* We otherwise fear being judged for our mistakes; for our poor choice of words and phrases; for expressing too many opinions; or for making errant comments that might offend. We build trust in our communications in the same way we built trust with those we taught to play catch. We are always on our guard against conflict, always careful with our intentions, and try not to be unprepared when something is thrown in our direction. We think we know with whom we have to pitch underhand and with whom we can play hardball. The official rule of both games: *Make no attempt to hurt the other.*

You will know when you have overstepped the unwritten rules of the game when others are offended with what you've thrown at them...or if you become offended with what they've tossed at you. You aren't always sure what others are thinking when you are playing the game, but you can be absolutely certain that conflict is present when your partner threatens to *take the ball and go home*. Communication requires that *the ball remains in play.*

This "ball" analogy can go a long way to understanding conflict. Let's say that I return home after a road trip and walk into the house to find my wife standing in the front hallway waiting for me, arms folded tightly across her chest, her expression grim, lips tightly held together and that one foot tapping impatiently against the floor. I am the first to "toss the ball" even though I am keenly aware that this would not be the posture of a person preparing to "play."

> *"Hi, it's good to be home. How are you?"*
> **"Fine!"**
> Knowing she is obviously not fine, I pick up the ball and toss again.
> *"You OK?"*
> As if frozen in place, she repeated, even louder, ***"I said I was!"***
>
> **An Aside:** If you remember nothing from this chapter, remember this: When the ball is "in play," the individual receiving the pitch will *always*... that is *always*... have two, and only two, choices. She or he will **accept or escalate**. In this instance, she could *accept* by passing the ball back and saying why she is so upset... or she can choose to *escalate*... attempt to control me to say or do whatever it is she believes will correct whatever it is that she is thinking, but not sharing, that has her so angry.

What she is now choosing to do is *escalate* with: ***"I said I was FINE!"*** She had the ball; all she had to do was toss it back so I might know what terrible deed warranted such a reception. Instead, by escalating, what she is doing is throwing the communications ball over her shoulder and saying, ***"Go chase it!"***

> **An Aside:** When your spouse knows what is wrong but is not willing to share it out loud, isn't that a lot like saying, ***"If you loved me, you'd know what I was thinking?"***

I, too, now have the same two choices; I could *accept* that I obviously have forgotten to do something and wait for the ball to magically appear, or I could *escalate* this… choosing to take it another level. Instead of trying to find out where the ball was hidden, what if I escalated with: *"Great! If everything is fine, what's for dinner?"*

If she realizes that I haven't a clue what this is all about and she alone knows where she has hidden the communication ball, she could now end this by choosing to <u>accept</u> rather than continuing to <u>escalate</u>. If, however, she now has too much emotion invested in this to "back down," she will stand behind her pride and choose again to escalate. I will know within seconds her decision. Here is the wind up… and the pitch; **"I'm going home to mother!"**

I, too, decide to *react* (not to be confused with *responding*) and escalate with: *"Have a nice trip!"*

> **An Aside:** When both parties volley like this, each secretly hopes that the other will be the last one holding the ball. *"I won't have to lose face if YOU will be the first one to put the ball back in play."* Pride can be a formidable hurdle to overcome, huh?

The game can end at any time: I could have held the ball when it was tossed and said: *"You are obviously angry, please tell me what has you so upset."* In turn, instead of throwing the ball at my head when I first walked into the house, her first pitch could have been: **"You forgot to take out the garbage and the dog made a mess all over the kitchen!"**

Yes, Communications is *exactly* like playing ball.

The point is, *understanding* is critical to open communications. We cognitively accept the premise…but only as long as *others* are willing to accept *us*…first! We think every conversation, every opportunity to relate with others, every comment tossed in our direction, every word or inference…is *"all about me."* We guard against revealing *too much* for fear that we might be judged. (We know of this fear because we are so quick to judge others by how *they* look and by what *they* say).

More often than you would care to admit, while the person across from you is speaking, your efforts to communicate become more of an exercise at *pretending* to be listening. As you attempt to listen, your mind races to relate to what you're hearing. You are reminded of similar experiences. In the length of a heartbeat, your mind conjures related images, you determine if the speaker is "right or wrong," you place value and worth on what is heard, and you infuse your own perceptions and understanding as the story you're hearing unfolds.

Rather than listening, and responding in turn to what you are hearing, you tend to focus more on what *you* are going to say when it is your turn. Your motive in seeking understanding really seems to be, *"I just want YOU, to understand ME."* Even after you have injected your comments into what is now a conversation, you replay what you just said in your head... judging your own words and actions against your intent (even as you are judging and interpreting your speaker's words, actions, and intent). After you rewind the conversation, you can't wait to insert into the next break what you "should have" said or done, and what you "ought to" do or say *next time* to make sure they *"understand, accept, and affirm me."* (It's hard to listen, when you're not listening... isn't it?)

You are going to want to sit down for this next part. In your on-going quest to meet your need for the *"understanding of me,"* that person standing across from you is doing *exactly* the same thing. Both of you are trying desperately to meet your *independent* Needs to be accepted and affirmed. Both parties in chance meetings or purposeful conversations secretly insist on being the first one to be understood, accepted and affirmed. Both try to shove their message on the other at the same time. Both exert limitless behaviors and attempts to control... at the same time... to get those signals out there. How often do we fail to grasp the concept that we are not the only person in the conversation, relationship, negotiation, classroom, sale, family, etc., trying to send that message? How productive is it to try to pour water into an already full bucket? How can you hope to fill another "full bucket" with what you have to say if he/she is also...pardon the expression... still full of it?

You know those times when you were sure others "got it," when others *DID* affirm, accept and understand you? Once your needs were met...and *only* after you were sure they *got the message*...did you feel the pressure lift. For in that moment, the quest was over. In that moment, only *after* your Need to be heard was met, were you finally ready to give back what has now been offered to you: Understanding.

It's not very flattering, of course, but visualize every person you meet as being full of emotions. That is, think of every person you meet as a bucket full of the *same* human Needs for love, respect, acceptance, fun, freedom, and understandings that YOU have. The pressures of work, the obligations of family, the weight of personal responsibilities, the same daily frustrations and anxieties of life that you feel...every other person you meet feels that too! The most effective way to *receive* understanding from others, therefore, is to *first* allow others to be understood; to *first* allow others to "pour out" some of what they are carrying. Until you allow others to "dump" some of what is in their bucket *first*, they will not have any room in their bucket to receive anything from you.

The lesson, therefore, is to be patient; be the first to allow the other to "dump." When it is your turn to pour from your bucket, you will know immediately. His words, inflection and body language will say to you, *"Thank you for allowing me to get some of that out of me. Now, allow me to receive from you."*

A Final Thought:

ALL humans have a Need to be AFFIRMED and fulfilled; to be heard and truly understood. This is one (of five) of our basic human Needs. Understand that every behavior you receive from others is simply each person's best attempt to meet their own basic human Needs. Once you make the decision to be more attentive to the Needs of others, then the pressure is off in trying to compete for understanding. By first yielding this courtesy to others (and this will be evident through words, inflection and body language), you will read in others that they, in turn, will be open...and willing...to understand and relate to YOU. You will discover that others will actually begin treating *you* differently, more positively, and they won't consciously realize why they're doing it… guaranteed.

What would happen if you took the risk to meet this Need to be heard in others? What would happen if you adopted the *attitude* to offer others the opportunity to be *understood*...first? You already do it in so many other ways everyday. What would naturally happen if you attempted to pass through a doorway at the same time another person is trying to enter? Without prompting, the one slightly ahead of the other will pause, smile, and hold the door open for the other person to pass through that doorway...first. The one holding the door open is rewarded with a *"Thank you"* for his/her thoughtfulness, while the other is acknowledged in return, verbally or with a nod or smile, with a clear message that says, "*You're welcome.*" In that instant, another step has been taken in the quest for understanding as two total strangers have momentarily connected in a common-union to meet each other's needs. True communications is exactly like this: it is *keeping the ball in play* with our words, inflection and body language.

Chapter 3

Rumors:
The Absence of Understanding

*"Sticks and stones may break your bones...
but words can never hurt you."*—Mom

Mom was wrong. Rumors, i.e., gossip, slander, and malicious lies, can divide relationships, devastate teams, dissolve a marriage, end a career, dash hopes, ruin your business, destroy your health, lead to depression, and even to the finality of suicide. No, mom, telling your kids to ignore the pain of rumors won't take the hurt away: *"Sticks and stones may break your bones...but rumors will break your heart."*

Rumors and gossip may not exist where you live, but they do everywhere else on the planet. These rumors are composed of words...just words. No sticks, no stones to break your bones. Are rumors just idle comments— veiled attempts to control? Are they angry retorts to save face? If they are just words...how bad can it be?

Words can bring a smile or heartbreak; they can be encouraging, or dash your hopes; they can lift your spirits or tear you apart. Once unleashed, a rumor grows legs and takes on a life of its own. This is the *rumor mill* you've heard so much about. You will choose, at either a conscious or subconscious level, to be a part of the cycle of gossip that swirls around you... or not. That is, you will choose either to be a player in this on-going drama, or to step aside and let it continue on without your participation. In a seminar series that seeks to understand, accept, and resolve conflict, it's important to take a few pages in this book to reexamine the impact of rumors.

While rumors may contain some elements of "truth," rumors cannot substitute for, nor are they – truth. Rumors seem to be made up of perceptions of truth, inklings of facts, a sprinkle of excitement, and a trace of the cloak and dagger. Mix in a dash of the controversial, images of the confessional, equal amounts of surprise and indignation, and rumors are born. Those starved for understanding and acceptance, anxious to know "the truth," mark the hapless subject of a rumor as *guilty* and often before he or she is aware that they were even on trial. An individual's actual guilt or innocence takes a backseat to the seeds of doubt now planted in the community and shared by all those "in the know." Any attempt on the part of the subject of the rumor to respond to the many versions of 'truth" now being spread across the community, will now be seen only as defensive remarks intended to cover up *the real truth.*

> **An Aside:** You've got to love that oxymoron *the real truth.* When you pick up this catch phrase in a conversation, imagine little red flags flying over the head of the speaker. These are clear indicators that you are in the presence of an official "rumor mill" operative. The clue is in the implication that there is somehow more than one truth and this person now has the *real* stuff. There will always be differing versions of what may have…or may not have happened. Everyone will bring their own experiences, their own perceptions of how life "should be" into every situation. Because there will always be more than one side to a story, there will always be more than one perspective – more than one way to see "the real truth."

When you are on the receiving end of a rumor (otherwise known as gossip), you are being asked to buy into something that may or may not be based on fact. More than likely, it is based on something like this: *"I heard it from Mary, who heard it from Julie, who heard it at the mall, so it MUST be true."* Is this the real measure of the r*eal* truth? If a tale was told more than three times it MUST be true? (This is what your mother probably meant when she told you to *"consider the source."*)

Mother probably also told you to be wary of wolves in sheep's clothing. The combination of the words *the real truth,* first and foremost, is the speaker's intent to tell you that he (she) is *"in the know"* and you are being privileged to be hearing this information. He is also telling you: *"See how important I am? You should be grateful for this knowledge."* And, more importantly, *"Because I am telling you what really happened, you are not to pay attention to any subsequent explanations or anyone else's rumors."*

Because we place *so* much emphasis on the interpretation of words to understand the intent of others, it is apparent that we place more trust in words, than in people. Many of us readily accept whatever we *hear*, make instant judgments, provoke conflicts, even end relationships based solely on the words that are placed in front of us. We do it, oddly enough, to meet our own Need for peer acceptance, but how cowardly it is to put others *down* for the sole purpose of lifting ourselves *up*. As long as we put more trust in *words*, than we do in *people*…those whose acceptance we inherently need… we will continue to empower conflict and grant permission for other *words* to rule our relationships: words like *mistrust, misperceptions, misunderstandings,* and *miscommunications.*

A Final Thought:

Rumors: We love them… we hate them. We *love* to take a part, to hear it all, to be the first one on the block to "know" the guff on our neighbors. Yet, YOU have been overheard to say, *"how unfair it is"* and how you *"hate it"* when you are the topic of that rumor. That pain is real, isn't it? So why do you persist in listening to and spreading what you hear? This is oversimplified, of course, but you listen because you don't want to lose the Acceptance of your peers; those who bring you news from the darkness of the rumor mill. Do you feel secure in conspiring against others because you foolishly believe that what you say…and that which you allow others to pass on to you… will *"never get back?"* Do you hope that as long as you hide there in the dark, the one whose reputation you are standing on will never know that *you, too, have been casting stones*? Have any rumors *about you* ever gotten back to you? How did that make you feel?

You can absolutely take this one to the bank: you can be certain, if that person who is so willing to run *to you* with tales of gossip and woe about others… she or he is also talking to others *about you*. The pull to be Love and Accepted is a powerful Need; but to *temporarily* gain acceptance at the expense of another is *permanently* trading your *integrity* to get it. Is it worth it? On what… or on whom… do you stand on this subject?

Chapter 4

Intra-Personal Behaviors: Establishing the *Need* to Listen.

"So, what's in it for me?"

Experience (memory) is a marvelous teacher. It really does allow us to recognize a mistake… immediately after we make it again. Experience also allows us to instantly recall those moments when life takes our breath away; the first time you laid eyes on your newborn child, those walks on the beach, the baby's first steps, or the first time you saw the gleam of moonlight reflecting across the lake. All moments, good and bad memories, will be stored for life. When frightened or shocked, you can even freeze a memory, having it available for immediate recall; like where you were when JFK died, when the space shuttle exploded in midair, or the towers fell on 9/11.

Many other special moments also hold emotional attachment. Like the times you were picked last in gym class, screaming with your friends at the fun house, the shock of losing a loved one, or even times of personal recognition and celebration. Unless too severely traumatized by the event, such moments that bring exceptional affirmation or rejection will remain "fresh" and available for instant recall until you die. As opposed to the *Inter*personal behaviors you act out, these are the *Intra*personal thoughts that you relive only within yourself.

One of the more positive memories I took away from my three years in the seminary was this whole concept of service. From a very early age, I created the mental picture that service was an *action*; something to do. I often tagged along beside my mother as she carried soup or dinners to the elderly neighbors. How many times had my cheeks been pinched and my head patted when my folks insisted that I go along on those visits to the nursing home? The smell of hot rolls when we came home from school usually meant someone died, and we knew these would be going to somebody else's house before we had dinner that night. And I knew I'd be cutting another lawn for free when my parents said, *"Mr. or Mrs. So-and-So are too old or too ill to cut their own grass."* No, the concept of service wasn't a foreign subject in my house.

I can still visualize where I was and what I was doing the first time I heard this statement from Henry Noulin: "***Service isn't something to DO… it's someone to BE.***" A simple statement, but following a lifetime of experiences believing that service was an action… this one sentence had an impact that would influence me for the rest of my life. I finally *"got it!"* I knew immediately it would change forever the way I looked at people. It opened my eyes to an understanding that service places the Needs of *others* above self. Service is not an activity; to BE of service is a choice. Service wasn't an *action*…it was an *attitude*.

I share that story because this memory from my seminary experience is relevant in a book about Active Listening. It might help to establish the Need to listen as I believe there is a direct relationship between Service and Active Listening: **Active Listening is not something to DO… it is someone to BE.** It is choosing to **BE** present to meet this Need in others.

Active listening is BEING someone who will momentarily set his/her own agenda aside to meet this inherent basic Human Need in others. You ask, *"What's in it for me?"* By choosing to BE of service to another, to BE an Active Listener, you will *be* amazed at how others will begin treating you differently, more positively. They will do it willingly, they will do it for life, and they will do so without even realizing why they are doing it. This becomes the 'return' for choosing to place the Needs of others above your own. In this is the natural and positive consequence of your decision to BE present for others.

In education, since everything has to be "research based," let me offer you some interesting studies to support "listening." In one experiment, to determine if *plants could hear,* two identical terrariums were set up; each had the same kind of plants, and the same type of soil and nutrients needed to support each plant. Each received equal amounts of water and sunshine. On the end of each terrarium was a speaker so the plants could receive piped-in music. The only difference between the two was the kind of music introduced into each terrarium.

Mozart was piped into the first terrarium; into the other streamed hard rock. In the first terrarium, the plants grew strong and tall and flourished "listening" to Mozart. By comparison, the plants subjected to hard rock music grew for a time, leaned away from the sound, withered…and died. (That is about the same reaction I get with hard rock.) The experiment was determined to be *a success*.

Speaking of plants, whether we'll admit it or not, most of us really do speak to our plants. This next experiment was conducted to determine if our plants *"understood their environment."* In this study, as listening is fully 50% of communications, a plant was connected to a monitor to record the plants feedback during the study.

A device, similar to an EKG monitor for humans, was attached to the leaves of a plant and each time a human spoke to the plant the monitor was read. Initially, the botanist spoke to the plant in calm and soothing tones. Accordingly, a steady and rhythmic pattern was revealed on the monitor. Next, he raised his voice and yelled at the plant for not growing fast enough. Accordingly, the monitor reacted with jerky, erratic motions as if the plant might be fearful. Next, the botanist took a pair of scissors, walked slowly over to the plant and snipped a leaf in half. The needle jumped right off the chart! Wow! Think about *THAT* the next time you cut your grass!

In a more related human study, a slightly different survey was conducted to determine the extent of time the "average" employee engages in "verbal communications." The survey revealed that the average employee spends approximately three-quarters of his/her workday engaged in "verbal communication." Fully half of that time the employee is paid to do nothing but listen. In that time dedicated to listening only, the study indicated that the employee actually *missed*...didn't hear it, didn't get it, or didn't fully understand the entire message... three out of four times.

Putting that in terms we can all understand, let's say the average employee makes about...say...$40,000 a year. If three-quarters of the average employee's work day is to verbally communicate, then $30,000 is being paid to that employee to do just that...to be engaged in verbal communications. As 50% of communications is to "take in" what is being said, then fully half of that $30,000, some $15,000, is being paid to people to do nothing but listen to each other. But if the employee misses 3 out of 4 messages sent his/her way, then the "average" employee is taking home as much as $12,000 a year in *unearned* income.

So why is that? How is it that we hear...but do not listen? Why? WHY? I'd think that would be obvious.

From our earliest moments on the planet, someone was there to teach us that the world revolved around us. Think about your own children or grandchildren. As they grew up and we noticed their behaviors were becoming self centered and anti-social, we struggled to teach them to share, to "play nice," to be polite, to take turns, and not to constantly interrupt someone who is speaking. This is not training, this is an attempt at *retraining* after we had first confused the child by teaching him (her) that his entire world, did in fact, revolve around him.

Remember, all behaviors are *learned*. From birth our child *learned* that when she (he) cries, she'll get a bottle; she cries again, she gets her bottom dried, powdered and recovered; she cries again and like Pavlov's dog, we come racing back to rock her, to pat her, to play with her; she crawls out of the crib you tell her to stay in, and she is rewarded for not doing what you asked by letting her crawl into bed with you; she picks up a toy at the store and you say *No, put it back*...then you buy it for her; she wants fifty cents for a toy, you give her a dollar; she stomps her feet for ice cream, you certainly don't want her unhappy, so you buy it; she just *has to have* a cell phone... you say no...she cries, pouts, withholds affection (controlling behaviors)...so you rationalize that this will show her what a loving parent you are, and you get it for her. If the child complains about virtually anything at school, armed only with the child's version of events, you charge to the rescue...just as the child knew you would... ready to lynch the teacher or principal for this *injustice* done to your child. Children do a far better job of training their parents than parents' do of setting boundaries and training their children. Yes, we *teach* our children to believe that all of life is *"all about me."*

The education system, of course, further perpetuates this *"all about me"* upbringing. Schools don't do it by giving the child everything he or she wants... we leave that to parents... instead, we have created an organized way to actually *teach* children that they do not have to listen. We teach them instead *only* how to talk, write and better express themselves… only half of the verbal communication skills that an effective, happy and productive life demands.

Through at least 12 years of school, teachers provide academics so that children can EXPRESS themselves. We teach children such formal classes as, grammar, reading, speech, theatre, debate, literature, oratory, creative writing…even creative dance and a dozen others forms of expression including keyboarding and technology skills. We have formally taught children to *express* themselves—how to be heard—ONLY. Without that other 50%, that other piece on how to listen, on *how* to be heard, we have, by design, not been teaching our students to *communicate*. We touch on it here and there, but how many of us… teachers or students…have had even the first semester class in how to LISTEN?

We cognitively *"get it"* that verbal communications requires equal parts of both expression and listening. Yet we are t*aught* only to express ourselves. Our mutually inherent human need is to be HEARD… yet we are taught only how to get *out of us* what we want to say. Consequently, as a society, we express ourselves quite well; we can read, write, and speak so that others understand. But we do not teach people *how* to be heard; how to allow *others to be heard*. As a result, misunderstanding, miscommunication, misperceptions, and Interpersonal conflict remain a way of life. We remain locked in a "me first" world where everyone has literally been taught to believe that my *"all about ME"* behaviors are acceptable.

If you don't believe this, watch the children on the playground. When children are speaking, are others actually listening? Instead of listening to each other, notice how all the children in the group seem to be talking all at the same time. In the classroom, how many dozens of times a day do you get this: *"Teacher, look at me. – Teacher, sit with me.—I had it first!—Teacher, listen to me read. – Give it back, it's mine!—-Teacher, come watch me.—Teacher, help me!—Teacher, Billy is touching me!"*

How about you? Your education and experiences have taught and reinforced in you how to express yourself, how to better articulate what you are feeling, how to express your hopes, loves, aspirations, accomplishments and dreams. You have literally been practicing for a lifetime how *to get it out of you;* to get others to hear you, to pay attention to you, to get you what you wanted. You have done this by refining Controlling Behaviors to get people to pay attention to you, i.e., stomping your feet, crying, feigning anger, pouting, withholding affection. You have been exercising and fine-tuning these behaviors since before you could crawl. All behaviors are learned… and all behaviors are choices.

You have these voices inside your head all of the time (relax, we all do) that are consistently working on you, planning and plotting as to how you can best express yourself. This is the incredibly human Need to be Affirmed: the Need all humans have to be heard. You are constantly trying to get others to listen to you *without* moralizing, lecturing, or offering unsolicited advice. You want to be heard completely and emphatically and this is perfectly natural. This is one of the five basic Needs *all* humans have in common.

Aside: Let's say you were outside working and became hot and thirsty. You began thinking about a way to quench your need for water. You went inside, headed to the cabinet and got a glass, moved toward the refrigerator, and poured yourself a much needed drink of cool water. The instant that water hit your lips, the anxiety you weren't even aware you were feeling began to abate. The sensation of satisfaction and relief became conscious thoughts. Whatever else was going on around you at the time became secondary to getting that glass of water… and meeting this Need. You had always taken water for granted, for water is after all, as common as, say, the people around you. Yet when you really needed that drink, you were aware just how focused you had become on getting that Need met.

In the same way, maybe you've been taking the Need to be Heard (Affirmed) for granted, too. Many of us simply assume that just because we have something to say, that someone would *naturally* be there to meet your Need. Other than your minister or therapist, how easy is it for you to find someone who will truly LISTEN to you? Keep in mind… there is no basic human Need to Hear; the Need is to be HEARD. Work to meet this Need in others…and others *will* trip over themselves to listen…to be there… for you.

When my sons were in elementary school, Irene and I took the boys over to the nursing home a few blocks from our house. Most of the residents were short on family, so during the summer, our family was family for many of these residents. We sought out the folks we had established relationships with and made sure we saw them during our visits. Mrs. Emerick was a former school teacher; she could recite more poetry from memory then I think I ever read. Mrs. Urskin taught my youngest son what the inside of a library looked like because our assignment was to go to the library to bring her new reading books each week. Rose was one of my favorite folks to visit. She was a lonely, sad lady who told me virtually the same story every time we sat down together. She related to me the loss of her husband, the falling out with her church, the separation from her daughter, and the pain of having her grandchildren held hostage from her by the daughter. She anguished over the pain of growing old and not being permitted to see her grandchildren. Week after week, over and over again, she told me the same stories. Yet, week after week, before I left, she would say, *"Thanks for coming. You really listen to me."*

Nine year old Stephanie sat in the funeral home as her mother stood beside the casket being consoled by people this little one didn't know. They were saying goodbye to her grandfather. I sat down with Stephanie and listened to her struggles and with what the loss of her granddaddy would mean to her. We also talked about her school, her collie named Fancy (she stayed outside because she "wouldn't wipe her feet") and other aspects of life important to a third grader like the difficult decision as to which boy to choose as her boyfriend, Alex or Timmy.

Her mother came to me later that evening and said, *"Thanks for entertaining Stephanie."* My own sister said, *"It looked like you were really getting into that conversation with Stephanie."* I found both of their comments to be odd. Both of them saw Stephanie as someone to be amused. Just because she was smaller, younger than the rest of us, how could they miss the fact that children were people, too? The littlest among us are more insecure, in constant need of love and acceptance, and are always struggling to be heard in a grown-ups world. Children desperately need to be heard, too. Stephanie and I became fast friends and pen pals. In case you were wondering... she picked Alex.

When my sons were playing soccer, I participated with them by becoming a soccer referee. During a break between games, I was standing at the concession stand when another referee came over and started talking. Other than the fact that we were both dressed in black, we didn't appear to have much in common. I had never met the man before, but in only a few minutes, he began sharing about his impending divorce, the pain this was causing him and his anxiety over what this would do to his family. Almost as abruptly as this conversation started, he literally stopped in mid-sentence, developed that deer-in-the-headlights look and said, *"I have no idea why I'm telling you all this. You're just so easy to talk to."*

Such stories are not unique and they are certainly not unlike similar experiences you could relate when someone opened up to you; when you were willing to put your own agenda aside to realize the impact listening has on another. Such examples serve as first hand testimony to the impact *you* have had on another when you were willing to temporarily empty yourself, to put your own agenda aside *to BE of service* to another. These moments are not staged, scripted, or planned. They are not common, nor do they occur without your consent. Yet, while these moments, these snapshots in time, cannot be measured, tasted, or touched, the world may never be the same because of them... because of you. For in the hearts and minds of others, for that moment, *you* were willing to do something few others in their lives were willing to do: *"Listen to me!"* You provided some of what they Needed; you did it without judgment, without moralizing or lecturing. You put aside your own agenda to meet their inherent, basic human Need to be heard.

And it won't end there. You will soon realize just what an impact such moments have on others when *you* first demonstrate, "I'm LISTENING!" While you might not have given these occasions to BE of service to others a second thought, the one who was *being* heard...will. Each time you are willing to actively listen... to meet this Need in others...it subconsciously becomes, in the minds and hearts of those who were heard, another stepping stone in a pathway that will always lead them back to you. They will remember that *you* were there when they needed someone to *"Listen to me."* It is as certain as sunshine that when you first work to meet this Need in others, others *will* go out of their way to meet your Need. They will do it willingly and eagerly. They will realize only that in *your* presence, they found rapport... they experienced emotional relief... they were not judged... and they were heard.

So who do YOU go to when *you* need to be heard? Who do you seek when you want to share the details of the most important person in *your* life: your fears, your joys, your excitement, your accomplishments, your pain, your sadness, your loneliness, your loves, your...? You don't pick just anyone to hear the workings of your inner heart, do you? You pick someone you believe you can relate to, someone like you, someone who will not moralize you, judge you for your mistakes, offer unsolicited advice, or above all, someone who will not betray your trust by telling your secrets to others. How easy is that person to find for you? How easy is it to find someone who will BE present for YOU?

A Final Thought:

You may not be the next Ghandi, Mother Teresa, or Martin Luther King, but if you are willing to listen, to relate, to extend your trust, to withhold judgment, to empathetically, completely and actively listen to another, the world will never be the same because of it. As we move through this book, if you practice these simple strategies as to how you can BE present for others, you will be amazed how others *will* begin treating you differently, more positively, and they will go out of their way to BE present for you...guaranteed.

NOTES

Right now, at this moment, you are thinking of someone with whom you want to have a better rapport. If the first move is up to you, what steps are you willing to take to renew that relationship?

Right now, in this book, on this page, write down what you are prepared to do.

Section 2

Obstacles to Listening:

A wife shouts this to her spouse, a frustrated teen yells at her parent, and when the teacher lost control, the teacher, too, wants to know, "Why won't you listen to me?"

Chapters

    5 IT'S ALL ABOUT ME: How we process thought

    6 ONE ON ONE: Our agenda gets in the way

    7 IN GROUPS: We behave differently

Chapter 5

Obstacles to Listening: "It's all about ME"

EWE.

"I think, therefore... I am confused."

A man was walking in the woods and came upon a bear. Surprised, the man immediately backpedaled, slipped on a rock, tripped over a log, fell over the hill and broke his leg. While he was lying there, unable to run, the man looked up to the top of the hill and saw the bear looking down at him. He began to pray: *"Lord, please save me from that bear. Lord, I need a miracle here. Lord, please turn that bear into a Christian!"*

At that moment, a miracle happened. As the man watched, the bear immediately fell to his knees, put his paws together and growled, *"Lord, thank you for this meal I am about to receive."*

The moral of the story? Be careful what you ask for. When you ask another to *"please listen to me,"* prepare yourself, for seldom will you get what you asked for.

Experience has taught me that before people are ready to become engaged, empathetic and active listeners, they first appreciate hearing some of the reasons why people don't, won't, or aren't listening. Do you want to know why *you* haven't always been as good a listener as you would have hoped? Do you want to know why others may not have always been listening to you?

In general, I'll lump these obstacles to listening into three separate categories:

It all begins from within; our *Intra*personal thoughts—Chapter 5.

Why our one-on-one conversations often fall on deaf ears—Chapter 6.

Why groups of people, e.g., our students in our classrooms, turn us off.—Chapter 7.

***Intra*personal: "It begins from within."**

Perhaps the most inherent obstacle to listening is in this fact: We humans can speak (depending upon which study you believe) between 100 – 180 words a minute, yet we can process thought from 450 to more than 600 words a minute... as much as 6 times faster than we can speak. It is not a fault, just a fact that your brain will not shut off. You can choose when to talk and when not to talk, but there is no ON or OFF switch to your brain; you are processing thought all of the time.

When you *hear* a story, or even a single word… *taste* that first sip of morning coffee… *see* a sunset, a tree, a dog, or new born baby… *touch* the first snow of winter or the fur of an animal… or when you *smell* homemade bread, the aroma of brownies in the oven, or the fragrance of a rose… the brain will instantly react to these triggers. Without conscious control, electrical impulses will instantly sort through the data base that is your brain to *bring back* related memories that you associated with whatever it is you just heard, saw, tasted, touched or smelled. Through our senses we are forever linked to our past. These are your *Intra*personal thoughts. These become obstacles to listening when we allow our thoughts to distract us from the moment at hand, from *listening* to the speaker. We can't stop our thoughts… we can only *direct* our thoughts.

To have the capacity to process thought is a miracle and one that is so complex that modern science still can't explain how it all works. We do understand which areas of the brain are responsible for different functions, but we can't duplicate it. To be able to process thought from what your senses trigger is a *gift*. Granting permission for yourself to be so easily distracted by your own thoughts… to be so willing to steal the focus from those with whom you were being asked to listen…is a *choice*.

For example, let's say I tell you about the new trick I taught my dog. Without another word being spoken, if you had a dog that could do a trick, saw a dog do a trick, read about dog tricks, or even knew somebody named Trixxy, YOU just had a flash back memory. Just that quickly, without further stimuli, your brain pulled that experience from your mental hard drive and it dropped that picture onto the monitor of your mind. You now can actually SEE that memory. Something in this example, a single word or description, reminded you of an associated experience. I repeat; that is a *gift*. Deciding to abandon the request to *"LISTEN to me,"* to instead follow your impulse to interrupt so you can inject what you are thinking… is a *choice*.

This thought process will happen without your conscious control. Sometimes, however, you will find yourself searching for just the right words with which to say whatever it is that just popped into your head; just the right moment to interrupt the flow of the speaker so you can enter into the "conversation." While you are still pretending to be listening, you are choosing just the right expression, just the right body language statement you want to make, and just the right moment to *break in* to say it. By choosing this tactic you can still hear, but you are no longer listening. You are now plotting behaviors for the sole intent of meeting your own Need to be heard.

The unfortunate part is, of course, when you are doing all these mental gymnastics in preparation to get <u>your</u> message *out there*, you may have completely missed the intent of the message the person in front of you has been trying so hard to convey. Your speaker, of course, already figured out that you're not listening; he can see that in your body language. And this scene plays out hundreds of times a day. It is more than likely that you have been operating out of your non-productive habits for so long that you are probably not even aware that you are doing it at all.

Meanwhile, brace yourself, for just as badly as YOU want to be heard…your speaker wants to be heard, too. In the same way you are juggling what is *coming in* with what you want to *send out*… this is exactly what other people are doing while *you* are speaking to them. If you don't believe this… or if this still is not making any sense to you, think back to any conversation you were in, and recall how quickly YOU were interrupted with something like, *"You think THAT'S something, I remember the time I…"*

Children have very short attention spans…it can be measured in seconds!

You ask students to break into their groups. The children respond by jumping up, starting to talk to each other, dropping books, searching for the assignment, moving furniture around… at the same time *you* are attempting to provide directions. Next time, try, *"Eyes up here"*…then provide direction…then break into groups.

If you are a school teacher, notice how quickly your students are distracted… how quickly they *tune you out* when you say and do something like this: *"Ok, students, I'm now passing out the worksheet; get out a piece of paper and number down on the left side, from 1 to 24. On the right hand side, at the top, put your name, subject and class period. Get out your science books, turn to page 64 and begin."* Seemed like pretty clear instructions to you?

First, realize that every single one of the 25 students in your room are all unique, have differing levels of experiences, understanding, and levels of attention. All will demonstrate, in their own way, varying degrees of interest in you, their classmates and in your class. From the moment you began, *"Ok students, I'm now passing out…"* you lost them.

Some students had not yet "come back" from whatever Intrapersonal side trip they were currently taking to pay any attention to your latest instructions. Others heard, *"get out a piece of paper and…"* so they immediately stopped listening when they turned to their neighbor, who has also stopped listening to hear what was about to be asked, *"Can I have a piece of paper?"* Others stopped listening when they realized they didn't catch that part about *"…number down to what?"* Others, yet, are doing the same thing with different questions, *"What book?"* and *"What page?"* and *"What side of the paper?"*

Some simply didn't hear you because they had already reached under the desk to dig through the array of books, gum wrappers, notebooks, and assorted trash to find that science book. Bobby, who started flipping through the book already, looks over to Mary and says, *"Did you see that neat picture on page 24?"* Tommy got sidetracked on page 45 and exclaims, *"Hey, Johnny, did you know that frogs could do that?"* You lose them, you get frustrated, and you blame…*them*?

~The teacher looks over to Billy, who is looking down. *"Billy, please remember to turn in your homework."* Billy doesn't move. *"BILLY, your homework?"* Billy doesn't move. *"BILLY, I'm TALKING to YOU!"*

Billy jumps, startled, *"What?"*
"Turn it in."
"Turn what in?
"The homework!"
"What homework?"
"The homework I just asked you for."
"You didn't ask me for homework."
"YES, I DID."
"I was right here; no, you didn't!"

Billy was having a conversation when you interrupted him. Billy was having an *Intra*personal exchange. He was literally talking to himself. This would be no different than if Billy had been in dialogue with another student. In this case, he was already in discussion with the most important person in his life. He was not focused on anyone else. The teacher was trying to talk with him at the same time he was in 'conversation' with himself. He was jarred back to the present when the frustrated teacher said, *"BILLY, I'm TALKING to YOU!"* All the boy heard was "BILLY…" as the rest of the sentence, or any previous statements in the room hadn't caught up to him yet. Having already been engrossed in thought and now rudely interrupted to come back to the here-and-now to pick-up what he missed, Billy's natural retort was, *"What?"*

A Final Thought:

In every example noted above, students asked for the instructions to be repeated. Can Interpersonal Conflict begin this easily? Absolutely! The frustrated teacher finds herself saying, *"I already told you; you should have been listening!"* Conflict rages as both the teacher and her students wonder why. Such scenes are repeated dozens of times a day, everyday in the classroom. The children were processing… in their own ways. Instead of beginning by asking for the children's attention, the teacher immediately jumped into the directions. Because the teacher was ready to *speak*… because *she* had something to say… she assumed the students "should be" ready to *listen*.

Is there a need to understand the *need* to listen? Hmmm.

Chapter 6

Obstacles to Listening: "One-on-One"

"Never assume that others will hold the same level of awareness, the same level of attention, the same enthusiasm for the topic, or the same interest for YOU or your class...as YOU do."

Years ago, I remember reading about a survey provided to employees in more than 1000 companies within the United States. When asked what the greatest concern was in their organization, the vast majority of the respondents considered their number one problem to be *"poor communications."* Is it possible that virtually every organization has the same problem? As diverse as companies and cultures are across this country, is it possible that *every* company is failing to adequately communicate with their people? Or is it more likely that every organization has something else in common: the independent *perceptions* of the employees?

Each of us has our own unique perspective on life. We each carry our own independent thoughts, perceptions, personalities, experiences and attitudes into the work place. Everyone wants to understand... we are obsessed by it... we think we always have to know *what's going on.* When we don't know something, we guess; we actually ask others... who also admit they don't know, but freely offer their own perspective and ideas as to *what's going on.* In the absence of understanding, all people will fill the void with speculation... with what we *imagine.* When the organization then offers information other than what was imagined, speculated, and rumored, we blame the organizations' *"poor communications."*

You already understand that our One-on-One conversations can be doomed from the start because of the Intrapersonal thought processes noted in the previous chapter. In one-on-one exchanges, other human dynamics are present. Your Need to be AFFIRMED must now be balanced with another of our five basic Needs: The Need to be ACCEPTED.

When you leave that world of Intrapersonal thought, your "all-about-me" world, and prepare to step into an Interpersonal "one-on-one" exchange, your ultimate goal is to be accepted; you want to be liked because you Need to be ACCEPTED. In conversation with another, your mind begins to reel with random, disjoined thoughts, planning behaviors, and asking questions… ALL so that you can get some of what you Need from this conversation. You will actually hear yourself asking, *Is my hair combed? I wonder what he thinks of this outfit. Did I tell him about that latest memo yet? What is he looking at? Is my lipstick on my teeth again? I hope I'm making a good impression. He has a nice smile! Must be careful; can't show too much interest. This is dull. Time to nod again like I actually care. How do I end this? Did he just say that? Did I put money in the meter? That reminds me of…*

This thought process is not only going on inside YOU… this is the same erratic, non-stop thought loop that is flashing at high speed through the mind of the person standing across from you, too. The mutual interest you both have to meet your independent Need to be ACCEPTED is a natural barrier to focused communications; to listening to one another; and getting another Need met, the Need to be AFFIRMED (to be heard). You can choose to permit yourself to remain in this unspoken duel to be the first to get your Needs met… or you can choose to meet the Needs of others… first. Let's try a demonstration.

Imagine for a moment that your friend Martha just called and asked you, *"I'm having a problem and I need someone to talk to about this thing that is bothering me. If I come over there, will you help by listening to me?"* You are about to take your Intrapersonal thoughts into an Interpersonal exchange.

You say, *"Yes."*

The instant you hang up the phone, your mind will begin taking a mental inventory of that brief exchange. Your friend has decided that she trusted and respected you enough to ask *you* to be the one to hear about the most important person in her life. She asked only that you *"listen to me,"* so before she knocks on your door, *you* have a decision to make, too:

1. Will you… see this only as the opportunity you've been waiting for, to tell her what *you* think she wants to hear; what *you* believe she needs to hear? In fact, your first thoughts may not have been about your friend at all. Your personal goal is to get YOUR Needs met; to be ACCEPTED and AFFIRMED. You were only concerned with how you might be seen in her eyes if she comes over and you can't solve her problems for her. *"After all,"* you rationalize, *"if she doesn't want me to fix her problems, why else would she want to come over?"*

Your mind races then to prepare your responses: *"I don't want to let her down, to think I don't have the answers to what's bothering her; so if she is going to talk about her boss, well this is what I'm going to tell her. And if she is going to ask me about that project at work, I'm going to tell her what to do with it."*

On the other hand, maybe it doesn't matter what she has to say. Perhaps you have already determined that what you have to share is more important than whatever it is she has to tell you. After all, you need to be heard, too. So maybe you're already thinking: *"I can't wait to tell her about the new furniture I'm getting ready to buy."*

2. Or will you… do what you were asked: *"Will you listen to me?"* You could choose to say, *"She only wants to discuss what is bothering her. All she wants me to do is listen. What an honor it is that she would choose ME."* If this is what you choose to do, your intent will be to put aside your own agenda to focus on your friend. You need not prepare your answers… only prepare to listen. You can be at peace with this option because, *"She doesn't expect me to fix things for her; all she asked me to do was listen."*

> **An Aside:** When people are depressed, feeling rejected, disappointed, or otherwise full of emotion, they will seek out someone they believe can be trusted; someone they believe they can relate to… someone they believe who will *really listen to me.* Carl Rogers, the father of Rogerian Counseling said, *"People can and want to resolve their own internal conflicts. Often, all that is required is the willing ear of another; to allow others to give voice to thought so they can sort it out for themselves."*

Before Martha knocks on your door, to help you decide which option to take, you may want to ask yourself this: *"Is this an Honor… or an Opportunity?"*

Honor: If you accept this as a privilege, you will prepare to listen completely, set judgment aside, resist the urge to offer unsolicited, unwanted advice, and be careful not to steal the focus; careful *not* to bring the attention back to your own needs, wants and agenda. You may have already accepted that this may not have been an easy decision for Martha—to have selected you to be the one she has chosen to hear the details of the most important person in her life.

Opportunity: On the other hand, ALL people have that human need to be heard. Will you see this encounter only as an opportunity to be heard yourself? After all, you, too, have a story to tell; you want to offer advice, to tell others what they "should do" in virtually every situation, to console, to condemn or to otherwise make your own case, to sympathize or rationalize at what you are being asked to hear. Because you, too, want others to listen to you; to hear about *your* day, *your* grandchildren, your loves, *your* needs, *your* life.

How will you accept this situation where you have been asked to listen… as an *Honor or an Opportunity?*

Here she is… the knock on the door… it is Martha.

You welcome her in, exchange pleasantries, and soon sit down with Martha. Her body language will speak volumes to the burden she carries. IF you have chosen to do what she asked… to *"listen to me,"* you will literally be able to see the tension melt away, her posture begin to relax, gestures less forceful, the inflection less punctuated, even her breathing more natural. In allowing her to put *"voice to thought"* you are watching, in her physical appearance alone, some of the relief she sought.

A Final Thought:

In this illustration the key to understanding is an active, empathetic listener. Active Listeners set aside their own agenda, withhold judgment, accept the honor being offered and focus completely on the speaker. Picture the person asking to be heard as a vessel, a bucket full of… emotion. Always allow the speaker to "dump" some of what she (he) is carrying first. If you do not allow the speaker to pour out some of herself *first*, you can be certain that there will be no room in that vessel for anything that *you* may want to add.

Chapter 7

Obstacles to Listening: "In Groups"

"I suppose you're all wondering why I asked you here."

C.G. Jung, a one time student of Sigmund Freud, dedicated his life to studying the differences and similarities of man. He was asked what has become known as one of life's universal questions: *"Why do people act the way they do?"* His answer: *"Everyone wants to be accepted, to be made to feel a part of a peer group. Consequently, people will do what <u>other</u> people want them to do rather than what <u>they</u> want to do."*

This fear that we might lose Acceptance in front of our peers (*the Group*) is why we become defensive in front of the challenging student, are nervous when we must stand before our colleagues, and are apprehensive in front of strangers.

When we begin to feel comfortable with our one-on-one…our face to face discussions, we carry our Need to be heard to a larger audience. We carry it into Sunday school, the classroom, and the board room. We speak in front of the congregation, the faculty, workshop participants, and the administration. Anytime we become involved with a gathering of individuals (professionals, colleagues, strangers, parents or children), we move away from a one-on-one context of thinking to bring about the next step in understanding obstacles to Interpersonal communications: the "Group." The Group I'm referring to is *any* audience, or classroom, any collection of warm bodies, any segment of the population you are asking to *listen* to you.

For this writing, I am not as concerned as to your behaviors as a member of the audience. Nor am I concerned with your Need to be heard before the Group. The question here is why is it that people are *not* always choosing to listen to you whenever you are speaking, i.e. teaching or presenting, *in front of* the Group? Speaking *before* others is, after all, entirely different than speaking *with* others. You already know that as the teacher, you cannot be responsible for, or control, whether or not those who enter your classroom or audience will *choose* to listen. Conversely, however, you must also know that the teacher (presenter) has virtually *everything* to do with whether or not someone will *want* to listen after they get there.

The problem with uncovering some of the reasons why "the Group" isn't always listening to us, is that sometimes we don't always like what we find. It is, after all, far easier to project blame, rather than to accept the possibility that we could have some ownership for the miscommunications, misperceptions and conflicts that arise in our classrooms. My intent is to provide a better understanding as to some of the reasons why the Group won't listen to their teachers/presenters.

You wonder: *"Why aren't they listening to me? How do I get their attention?"*

Here are several reasons why the Group may not be listening to you:

1. *You* fear the loss of acceptance.
2. *You* know *they* are watching.
3. *They* want to avoid cognitive overload.
4. *They* want to be entertained, instantly gratified.

1. You fear the loss of Acceptance.

As we move through this, keep in mind that what you (and I) *Want* in this life is different from what we *Need*. Our wants begin as thoughts, desires or hopes. Our wants are motivated by one or more of our inherent, basic human Needs. Our behaviors are many, but our basic Needs are few: Love and Acceptance; Affirmation and Fulfillment; Fun; Freedom; and Survival. We want *things* or want to accomplish tasks so we choose behaviors that our experiences have told us will get us what we want in our lifetime pursuit to meet these Needs. We are constantly driven to satisfy these Needs through our choice of behaviors (see the Behavior Cycle page 19).

When you agree to speak in front of the Group, it is because of this basic human Need to be AFFIRMED (to be really listened to). As you prepare to speak in front of the Group the quest to meet this Need to be Affirmed will come into conflict with another Need; the Need to be ACCEPTED by your peers. Conflict will be present because you want so desperately to be Accepted that you will go to great lengths to avoid revealing too much about yourself. You will mentally exhaust yourself in efforts to conceal your weaknesses, inadequacies, or insecurities before the Group. The conflict you experience in your drive to fulfill your Need to be *Affirmed* by the Group, will be in direct proportion to the extent you believe that you have already been *Accepted* by the Group. Only then can you choose how much of your self you are willing to reveal to others.

Our **Students**:

Why do some teachers become openly defensive by the "bright" students in class, the ones that seem to challenge us to stay ahead of them? Some would say these students "keep us on our toes" while others see the same children as disrespectful or rude? Is it just because they test us, and we have to work harder to keep up with them? Or is it because we always have to be on guard with the ones that push us; on guard to keep them from looking beyond the image we project to avoid revealing the fears or inadequacies that lie hidden behind the mask?

To some degree, we all hide behind protective masks. We hold up these masks and defend them. We protect ourselves, shelter our egos against the judgments of others. It is perfectly natural. I thought Dr. John Powell said it rather succinctly as to why we do this: *"If I were to be completely honest with you, to reveal how I really feel... and you do not accept me... what else is there?"* Until *you* choose to accept *you*, both your strengths and your weaknesses, you will choose to stay hidden behind your mask.

In these times of accountability in education, many teachers have been known to stiffen, to protect the masks at all costs. Rather than accept ownership for not being prepared, some teachers actually see the child's questions as attempts to trap them into openly revealing what is already obvious to the rest of the Group. With the challenging child, you may be the one who has chosen to become defensive. When the child gets too close to the truth, the reality may set in that you failed to set clear boundaries in this classroom, or that you are not fully prepared this day to teach, or perhaps you can no longer conceal the fact that you simply don't care. (As one teacher told me, *"I get paid the same whether I care or whether I don't... so why bother?"*)

To shield against revealing weaknesses, some teachers will equate inquiry with inquisition and assign students detention for being *disrespectful.* They race to the principal to cry, "D*o something about that child."* Such teachers have been known to use sarcasm as a tack to *"keep them quiet."* Teachers use anger and raise their voices to deflect against having to admit being *uncertain*, or possibly *wrong* in front of the Group. As a last resort, they will use the power of the grade book to *put them in their place.* As long as we don't fear having to reveal what is behind the mask, we can maintain that air of superiority over children.

With our peers…with other adults…it is not that easy, is it?

Our **Peers**:

When you choose to stand behind the lectern at church, or walk in front of an assembly of your peers, your human objectives are the same: to be AFFIRMED and ACCEPTED by the Group. You will want to know what *they* are thinking about you.

Most school teachers don't give a second thought about standing in front of a classroom full of students, but they tremble at the thought of standing before a gathering of their peers. We do not feel threatened by children for this very reason because they are not our peers. Why does the trembling seem to intensify in direct proportion to the degree by which we perceive our audience to be equal or superior to ourselves? If you don't see your students as "equals" perhaps you are not as concerned as to what they think of you. Yet when you speak in front of your peers…in front of those for whom you NEED their love, respect and acceptance…you will always want to know: *"What do they think of me?"* Yes, your need to be AFFIRMED and your inherent Need for peer ACCEPTANCE is that strong.

Let's say you agree to speak before a group of your peers... now what?

It is perfectly natural that your mind will take side trips while you both prepare for...and then stand before...the Group. Your mind will wander off, leaving you in a cold sweat as it conjures up all sorts of scenarios for you to worry about; telling you what you "ought" to do, or "should" do about whatever you have allowed yourself to imagine. From almost the very moment you agreed to speak before the Group, your mind began reacting (not responding) to nature's 'fight or flight' fears that have overcome you as you prepare to speak...to *them*. Your stomach tightens, you begin talking to yourself (often out loud), you waste time wondering how you got yourself into this, you try to find answers to the "shoulds" and "oughts" of what *could* happen, you actually consider which excuse sounds the most plausible when plotting how to cancel this and still save face.

Thoughts of doubt and fear set in long before you actually step up to the stage and stand before this group. But you made it this far. Your name is called and you step to the podium . *"Careful, don't trip!"*—*"I should have worn the blue suit!"*—*"Did I lock the car?"* You walk nervously, ttaking inventory on the way: *"Hair combed? [check]; Shoes polished? [check]; Dandruff off my collar? [check]; Fly closed? Fly closed?!? Should I look? Fly closed!" [check]*

You now make it to the podium. You thought you were nervous anticipating this moment; you are now standing in front of this group. You want your peers to like you, to respect and accept you. You look into that sea of faces and instantly your mind shuts down: you lose your focus. Suddenly, everything you rehearsed, all that practice, seems to have been in vain. If you have allowed yourself to believe that YOU are more important than the message, your mind will go into overdrive:

"Maybe I should tell them about my airplane ride to get here? Yeah, other speakers do that. Don't let them see your legs shake! Slow down! Did I really say that? Quick, say something clever so they don't think you made a mistake... like, 'Oh, well, what do you expect for a Monday?' or 'It's been a long day already.' Yeah, that's original! That guy is reading a newspaper, am I that boring? I can't believe I just said that! I hope they like me."

And on it goes...on and on... *"Why is she looking at her watch? Those two are talking...I'm sure they're talking about me. Do I look nervous? I just stumbled over that word...better make a joke to cover up my mistake. Oh, no, I didn't plan for that...now I just forgot my line! Quick, fill the silence with something; something really clever like, "UH" or "AND UH," or "YA KNOW?" Yeah, keep saying that when you have nothing to say and no one will ever figure out you're stalling, wasting their time, while you try to find something of substance to fill the silence."*

The truth of the matter...with children or with your peers...the bottom line is this: you must first choose to accept yourself if you expect the Group to accept you. The more you can accept your own strengths and failings, the more comfortable you'll become before the Group...any Group. Conversely, the less accepting you are of yourself, the more you will project your fears and insecurities into your audience.

If you cannot accept your weaknesses, you will *imagine* that your students/ participants will not accept you (and your faults), either. You will no longer be presenting, but *performing,* before the Group; trying to meet the expectations of the Group by trying to outthink what you *imagine* they are thinking about you. At this point, you have lost your focus; you have now granted permission for the Group to determine your personal worth. This is the moment when you have allowed the *messenger* to become more important than the *message*. This is now all about you. You can now realize that your fears and discomfort before the Group are not imposed by your audience...they are self-imposed.

The next time you are asked to present a message before other adults, when you feel that knot beginning to develop, the cold sweat form on your brow, and that *"what am I doing here"* sensation taking over your emotions, keep this simple thought in mind. In fact, if you remember nothing else from this chapter, this book, or perhaps from this series, repeat this sentence to yourself the next time you agree to speak before your peers: *"This presentation is NOT about ME. The message is always going to be more important than the messenger."*

Since the early 1980's, I have traveled extensively, literally from Green Bay to Tampa Bay, speaking before hundreds of classes, organizations, schools and school systems. I have spoken with groups of dozens to groups of thousands. To this day, I honestly cannot remember a time...a single time...when I failed to silently recite this to myself before walking into a school classroom, onto a stage, or before an auditorium of my peers. *"This presentation is NOT about ME. The message is always going to be more important than the messenger."*

2. You know *they* are watching:

Your role as a presenter/ teacher in front of the Group is two fold: to help the Group increase their interest in the presentation *and* to remain focused on the message. You can't do a thing about what they bring to the Group; you *will* influence what they take away. There are a number of reasons under this heading why the Group might lose interest, tune you out, or otherwise choose not to listen to you. You can use the anagram **C.A.M.A.C.** if you want to remember these:

C: Is your audience COMPELLED to be here? Before you step before any audience, first do your homework to determine if this is a Friendly – Neutral – or Hostile audience? If this is a *friendly* group, they want to hear more about this topic, have heard something positive about you or the presentation and will assemble willingly to participate; *neutral* crowds will assemble, either voluntarily or directed to, but they are still open.

The *hostile* crowd is where someone has an axe to grind. They may have heard about the presenter, the presentation, the topic, have some other agenda, or otherwise, clearly do not want to be here. They are compelled to be here...they would prefer to be somewhere else...and they are not bashful about letting you know just *how much* they don't want to be here. Some participants may "act out" to call attention to themselves. In this way, they will be satisfied that whoever ordered them here will know of their discontent. And that is actually the good news—this means it is *not* about you.

A. They will ANTICIPATE what you are going to say. Some members of the Group will stop listening in mid-sentence to mentally finish sentences for you. For example, imagine telling the Group: *"When he was just a boy, he chopped down a cherry tree in his yard. When he was asked about it he said, "I cannot tell a lie, I did it." Where did this happen?"* Somewhere through that you began searching through your mental data base, found the answer and exclaimed: *George Washington*!

If you were listening (and not reading) while you processed the question, you inserted the name *George Washington* into the sentence. It is a perfectly natural act to hear part of a sentence and anticipate what the answer would be. You did that because your mind can process thought as much as six times faster than the presenter can speak. But when you are processing, you are not completely listening. While you were processing the answer, the sentence was completed. Because you anticipated hearing *who* chopped down the tree, you may have missed that the question was asking *where* did this happen?

Realizing that others will anticipate what is about to be said, you can understand why some people in the Group, though staring right at you, may not hear a word you're saying. This is perfect validation as to why the presenter needs to alter his/her delivery, inserting pauses, stressing main points, using movement, involving the Group, and utilizing inflection to better assure the audience will stay focused. Remember, the "average" employee misses 3 out of 4 things they hear, so repeating or rephrasing what you said is a very successful teaching strategy to improve listening...and learning. (You will notice this listening/comprehension strategy throughout this book where specific information in one chapter is reinforced/ repeated in other chapters.)

M. "The Group" will MENTALLY scrutinize you (your words, action and appearance). This is both a reason why they aren't always listening... and why you will remain so distracted, not always focusing on your presentation. You know that they are assessing...evaluating...yes, *judging* you all of the time. You know that because when *you* are a member of the Group, you do it, too, all of the time, judging the presenters and their performance. Now, as the teacher/presenter *before* the Group, when you look over *your* audience, you realize that each one of *them* is staring at *you*. They may be staring but their minds are reeling. The Group will assess... wonder... fantasize... and otherwise drift in and out while they appear to be awake, alert and conscious. You can't hear them, of course, but mentally they are saying such things as: *"I can't believe he is walking around."* or *"I wish he would speak louder."* or

"She has a nice smile." or *"I wonder if she really believes that?"* or *"I guess she is having a bad hair day."* or *"I can't believe he wore that tie with that suit."* or *"I wonder if he can cook?"*

The *good* news, it is perfectly natural, involuntary and harmless; you don't have to take it personally. The *very good* news is, you are not paranoid; you were right, they really are talking about you; they are *not* always doing it to be mean or spiteful; nobody is saying the same things; you can do nothing about what they're thinking; and this really is NOT about you. The *really very good* news is, you now know it's happening, and if you choose to, you can do something about it. The more interactive the lessons, the more the Group will participate and the less self-talk there will be to distract both you and them.

The bad news… whenever they are talking to *themselves* (and they are), these are the times when they are not completely listening to *you*. (Now do you understand why presenters…and writers…often repeat themselves? We want to make sure you get it. You get it?)

> **An Aside:** Speaking before a group of their peers is really traumatizing to a great many adults; it may be for you. As long as you continue to believe this is all about YOU, that *you* are more important than the *message* you are presenting, you will continue to be nervous each and every time you stand up before your peers. When the message and not the messenger becomes the spotlight, Group self-talk concerns will fade and your confidence will return…guaranteed.

A. Some will ASSUME that they know more about the subject than you do. People make assumptions in the absence of knowledge. Each participant must have enough information ahead of time to understand how this presentation will impact his/her own life. The Group also must know about the speaker. Participants don't really care what college you went to or that you live three states away. They want to know that you are providing something worthy of their time. They basically want to know two things: *"Do you have the experience or expertise to warrant my attention? And what are you going to tell me that I don't already know?"*

Teachers, for example, are a tough group. They don't want you to waste their time. Some members of this Group, for example, might assume just from the topic that whatever they need to do is more valuable than what they can get from you: *"Why should I be here? I've got papers to grade."* or *"We are preparing for the next semester; I should be getting my lesson plans ready."* In a workshop setting, how the topic and the speaker are presented to the audience can usually diminish this concern before the speaker says the first word.

An Aside: A note to presenters: From your first words…you will HAVE *them* or LOSE *them* in those first three minutes. Your audience will grant you these first three minutes…as a gift. Nobody really cares about your plane ride to get there…do not waste your first three minutes.

S. Many will not listen; only SELECTIVELY listen. Some members of the Group will SELECT what they want to hear…and close their minds/interest to hearing anything else. It may be the subject they disagree with, it may be the speaker they dislike, they got up on the wrong side of the bed, or they simply would rather be somewhere else, anywhere but here. Perhaps they just want to be heard and see this as their forum. If students/ participants are choosing *not* to listen, or to listen only to later take issue with what is being presented, this will become abundantly obvious. After all, what point would there be for selective listeners to *select* comments to disagree with, if they couldn't somehow let you know? A selective listener need not be confrontational, but there is really no such thing as *suffering in silence;* the presenter will soon pick up on the signals (as body language cannot lie).

Two days after presenting a session on Active Listening strategies to a school system in Florida, I got a call from a school official in that district who told me he couldn't wait to tell me this story. He was looking over the seminar evaluations when he said he read one that made him laugh out loud. *"This is classic,"* he told me, *"You've got to hear this one."*

As the session was focused on providing strategies for listening, he read me his evaluation: *"I really didn't want to be here so I was only half listening. About half way through I gave up and got pulled all the way in. I wasn't listening until then and now I wished I had been listening all along. Is he coming back?"*

3. *They* want to avoid cognitive overload:

Let's say you go to the theatre to watch a movie. How about, say, one of the Tom Cruise *Mission Impossible* movies. You are doing your best to follow along. As the many sub plots of the movie unfold the plot thickens and you want to know, *"Who did it?"* If you were able to watch the faces of those around you, you'd notice that one by one, they were *dropping out*; not everyone *getting it*. Some start to whisper, hoping their companion 'gets it" and will explain it to them; others collapse back in their seats; others shake their heads, fold their arms, or otherwise reveal through their body language the signs that they are "shutting down." With more information being introduced, more characters to remember, more details presented, you try to keep up with it all, too, when "it" happens. The frustration of *not* getting "it" kept mounting until the instant it hits you: *"I am hopelessly lost."*

Up to this point, your mind, like an electrical outlet, kept "taking in" more requests for "power." Your human quest to understand kept trying to make sense of it all. You were making your best attempt to respond to the mental demand to "get it." But electrical circuits eventually "break" as a container will eventually reach a level when it is full and can accept no more. When your mind reached the point of saturation, you have just taken in more than you could absorb; you will *involuntarily* give up and shut down. The abyss on the far side of that invisible threshold you just crossed is referred to as *cognitive overload.*

At the movies, you have only to wait and the plot will be revealed. In the classroom, however, there is no punch line. If WE give our audiences, the students in our classrooms, more than *they* can absorb, we lose them. And here, when that happens, there is no happy ending.

I remember my first computer. It was an Apple IIe. That computer had a finite amount of memory. When a disk could store no more, when it had reached its capacity, the screen would say DISK FULL. When too many files were opened at the same time… when too much was being asked of that computer… the entire screen went blank with the exception of a single picture: A BOMB*!* The computer seized; it shut down… without warning… in mid sentence…in mid-word! That old Apple computer had to be shut off and rebooted before it could again be brought back to life. Fortunately, unlike our computers, our students are kind enough to *act out* to provide some warning before *they* go into "overload."

In your classrooms, when you mumble, speak too softly, too fast, use too little inflection, provide your students with endless lists to remember, too many details, too much information, too many facts, or too many notes, your students will strain to keep up. Are you watching for the signs? The signs of "overload" are there, subtle at first: doodling, scribbling, excessive erasures, staring off into space or out the window, sighing, dropping pencils and books, shaking the head, flipping through papers, passing notes, head down, pushing the chair back, folding the arms, whispering, or otherwise, *acting out.* These are all clues, all examples of stressors that push our students (our Groups) closer to their cognitive limits. The mind races to keep up… but gives up. Once they cross that threshold, everybody loses.

If you can accept that the message is always going to be more important than the messenger, then you will want to make every effort to ensure that "overload" is avoided and that the message is being heard. Teachers and presenters who understand how the Group accepts information will have the greatest opportunity to retain their audience. While you can't always be successful at pulling in an uninterested or selective listener, you can, without a doubt, be responsible for turning off and shutting down an otherwise attentive Group.

Every classroom instructor learned in "teacher school" that children (all of us really) learn best when information is presented in groupings of 3-5 main points. We learned this technique to increase the rigor in the content, the retention of information, and our ability to apply deeper levels of understanding and analysis without overwhelming our students in the process. We learned that we could further provide relevance, offer significance to the content, by entering the student's world of understanding; incorporating into the instruction all three modalities… visual, auditory and hands-on.

We do this because we know that our audience's attention, their *inclination* to listen, is in direct proportion to their *willingness* to listen.

4. *They* want to be entertained (and instantly gratified):

In Memphis, Tennessee, I once had a parent come up to me after a conference and right after *"Hello,"* started asking a barrage of questions: *"Why won't my kid listen to me?* ~ *"How can I get him interested in school?"* ~ *"How can I get his attention?"* I told this parent that I would answer her questions if she would answer mine: *"How many forms of entertainment does your child currently possess?"*

She looked a bit puzzled, then looked to her 13 year old son who was standing beside her for an answer. The boy immediately began rattling off: "TIBO (and cable television), dozens of DVD's (and DVD player; one attached to the TV *"and the one I take to school."*), video games (and X-box), video tapes (and tape player), computer (table top with Web Cam), Internet access (unrestricted), two Ipods (because *"one was full, ya know."*), Game Boy (and cartridges), and a cell phone (plus the phone in his room). *And all this was in his bedroom.* He couldn't wait to add that he was going to get a "Wii" for his birthday (I'm still not too sure what that is).

The parent's eyes widened as the boy worked through his list. She was nodding her head before I could say a word. I made eye contact with mom and said, almost under my breath, *"Let's see, Dungeons and Dragons on-line with my friends... or my homework... hmmm?"* Mom smiled, mumbled *"I get it,"* grabbed Junior's hand and walked away.

The technology genie is out of the bottle and there is no going back. Every elementary child in America grew up with the Internet, yet many older Americans, parents and grandparents, grew up with Milton Berle on the latest technology in their age; a 13" box called a tel-e-vision. We come from different worlds, adults and children... literally. It is no wonder there are conflicts between parent and child, teacher and student. Seeking enjoyment through books and board games, puzzles, playing ball in the yard, or camping with friends seems a lifetime away from today's fast paced world. It might take... what... maybe hours to enjoy such activities to the end. Today, we have conditioned our children to believe that it is the adult's obligation to *"keep me happy."* You don't believe that? If the child is not kept active every minute... what is the next line you'll hear? *"I'm BORED!"*

How did it happen that we moved so quickly from rabbit ears to 1000 channels on *the dish*? From Atari to Game Boys; from postcards to E-mail; the library to the chat room; rotary dial to cell phones, palm pilot, and Ipods and blackberries; and when did "prime time" get replaced with "sexually explicit time"... all the time? What ever happened to Ozzie and Harriet and visits to Mr. Rogers' Neighborhood? It really wasn't all that long ago, was it?

In your lifetime, more advances have occurred in science, medicine and technology than any other time in the history of man. We can't expect our children to be less than prepared for this new era so our schools are doing their best to improve student learning, to adapt to a changing technological age, and to push children toward academic success. But there are other, less desirable changes that also impact a child's learning and development. Today, the number of single parent births is spiking, the divorce rate has broached 60%, and most traditional family households are seeing a rise in the number of adults in the home having to hold down two or more jobs just to make ends meet. All this has increased the pressure and stress on parents. This has translated to more day cares, extended family care, and "latch key kids" than ever before. The pressure of work and finances exerts multiple pressures on the adults… pressures that take a toll on the children as well.

While my back was turned, in the span of a single human lifetime, the world, indeed, has irreversibly changed. Thomas Friedman, in *The World is Flat*, paints an amazingly accurate picture as to how our world, now changing at light speed, moved from a world of walls, to one with no limits at all… *in the span of a single lifetime.* Even the expected norm for responsible parenting has taken a quantum leap, shifting such accepted roles of parenting from *entertaining* children, to constantly having to *keep* children *entertained*; from raising the child to become a *responsible* adult, to being the adult raised by an *irresponsible* child.

As adults we struggle to control our own fast paced and hectic lives *outside* the home, so how can we expect to control the fast paced and hectic lives of our children *inside* the home? When our children step outside, they see what other children have. Our children want what other children have. Since we believe this is what will *"keep them happy,"* and realizing if we don't buy it for them they could *"be mad at me,"* how can you say no? Do you think this "keeping them entertained," is a source of conflict between children and adults… between teachers and parents? Absolutely!

Children learned the meaning of *gratification* at a very early age. As all behaviors are learned and all behaviors are choices, we actually *teach* and *consistently reinforce* instant gratification to our children. From the pleasant comfort of a clean diaper to the warmth and satisfaction of the bottle, the child naturally grows to expect to be satisfied, to have his/her wants met. You are the instrument by which the child's wants are served. Like the proud parent you are, your world revolves around that baby. From the first smile to the first step, to the big deal made over the *big deal* made in the potty, you applauded virtually every positive behavior. You want all of your friends and relatives to make over the baby, too. Acceptance of the baby, after all, is acceptance for you.

By your actions, though innocent and well intended, you reinforce and condition the baby into believing that the world does, in fact, revolve around her (him). This expectation is modeled for the child with *your* behaviors. The baby cries and you pick her up; she grunts and points to something and quickly you run to get it for her; she bumps her knee she is rewarded with the "magic bandaid" and a hug; she smiles and she gets all the attention in the room; you say NO… then give in; you tell her she has to sit at the table until she finished her dinner… then let her go when she refuses; you ask her to pick up her toys then bend down and do it yourself; she throws the ball you tell her not to throw in the house, and breaks the lamp… one parent gets angry while the other confuses the child with a hug and says, *"oh, well, she didn't mean to."* With such conflicting behaviors, what are you *teaching* the child?

The first time, and *each successive time,* you fail to teach the child to accept ownership for his/her actions, or to acknowledge and support the natural consequences of behavior and the restrictions of boundaries, you reaffirm with that child… regardless of age… that consequence for actions *"do not apply to me."* You already taught the child that tears, pouts, and a sad face "work" on you (otherwise known as Controlling Behaviors), so the child continues to expect you to get what he wants. Soon, those *expectations* will become *demands*. Never doubt that children really do want (and need) structure (boundaries) in their lives. If not provided, they *will* demand it by acting out until it is.

Each time you have grown weary of giving in to those *"all about me"* acting out episodes from your child, you began by saying "No" or "No, I *really* mean it this time." or "If you do that *one more time*…" You then repeated yourself several more times, you said it in an increasingly louder voice each time, and you made sure you added arm waving and foot stomping to make your point. You did this because you realized that just "No" and the inconsistent threats and punishment aren't working anymore.

As you are escalating in your attempts to get *your* way… notice how your child's behaviors to control are also escalating. To get your attention now, what he is doing? He may have to pout longer, or cry louder, or jump higher, or hold his breath, bang his head, threaten to "run away," tell you he "hates you," or stomp his feet to make it perfectly clear that *"I am unhappy."* You have rescued him every other time from "unhappiness" so why should he believe that all of a sudden, you are serious about establishing and maintaining boundaries (structure) now?

If this is a familiar scene in your house *or classroom*, understand that all behaviors are learned. The child has been *taught* that *he can wear you down.* Remember the very first time you told your child something like, *"Pick up your toys?"* You got tired of waiting, so you picked the toys up yourself. The child knows that the first person to pick them up will be picking them up for life. You have just taught the child that he can *"out wait you."* It is with experienced certainty, therefore, that the "unhappy" child knows that *you* will eventually *"fix this thing that makes me unhappy."* You will do it because he knows he can wear you down… he can *out wait you.*

In his/her mind, that is what you do. *"I know you will, sooner or later, FIX "it"* (whatever IT is), take care of "it," make "it" better, or make "it" go away. *"I am not at all concerned with any cost or consequence to you."* The child's singular objective is simply to get his current *want* satisfied… and satisfied NOW. This is what the child has been taught.

While it starts in the home, it won't stop there. At home or school, on the playground, on the sports field, wherever, you race to defend her/him every time the child is faced with *unhappiness*. You don't even wait to hear what happened. All you want is to be rewarded with that smile again. You listen to her perspective and rush off in defense of your cub to *"make her happy"* again. At some level, of course, you realize this is not just about the child. You are getting something out of these rescues, too… or you wouldn't do it. You, too, need self gratification. To be rewarded with that smile again from your teen or preteen, rather than the usual mock indignation, says to you that you are loved and that *you* are surely a good parent. You say, *"See, my child is happy again."* When *my child is happy again*, MY Need for Love and Acceptance has been restored.

As the child gets older, if these enabling behaviors persist, you will continue to find some way to excuse his (her) behaviors, to defend his actions, and come to his rescue. By the time the child enters school, it is evident that the parent/teacher's goal of *"keeping me happy"* remains the same but the motivation may have changed. Parents and teachers still rush to bail out their children at this age because they don't want the child to be *"mad at me."* If the child is mad at me, he *"won't love me."* The parent might want to justify the child's behavior so as not to be socially *"embarrassed by my child's actions."* A divorced parent might rush to save the child because, *"I want the child to love me best."* Or the parent/teacher's Need for love and acceptance is so strong that with each rescue of the child, the parent/teacher is rescued and *"I will be elevated in the eyes of the child."*

> **An Aside:** As a school principal, I once had a parent come into my office to defend the actions of her child. Her opening remarks were, *"I won't have my daughter unhappy!"* As she attempted to justify why her daughter should not receive the consequence for her poor behavior choice at school, she actually said this: *"You have to change the rule. You don't understand.. You don't have to live with her. She can make our lives miserable!"*

If the goal is to raise a responsible adult, how long will the parent (teacher) persist in sheltering the child from consequence? If the child is not taught that actions have consequences, when the consequences are small and designed to teach life lessons and responsible behavior, then inappropriate behaviors *will* escalate as the child gets older. As long as this growing adolescent is taught that she will be sheltered from her consequences, who will she blame when her actions warrant serious consequences that the parent *can't* fix? What a disservice we do our children when we raise them to believe that *others* are to be held responsible for *their* happiness.

> **An Aside:** As a school principal, I remember the tenth grade student who had been struggling with math. His birthday fell two days after the end of the semester. Because he made a "C" in his Algebra course, his father wanted to get him *"something special"* for his birthday. He drove to school the following week in his brand new Mercedes 380SL convertible. Much nicer than any teacher's car on the lot, it was not an atypical example of the instant gratification this child had grown to expect. He expected it because the *parent* had taught and consistently reinforced with the boy that *"if I want it… I get it."* We could hardly wait to see what the boy would get for a graduation present.

I probably dedicated too many pages to making this point: *The Group* lives in a society where all have become conditioned to being entertained and instantly gratified. I am trying to address what so many teachers over the last decade have been wondering out loud: *"What happened?"* In the 'old' days, it was expected and even understood that students/audiences would willingly, respectfully offer their attention and parents would support the process by supporting the teacher. Today, the adult Group attitude is: *"Don't waste my time! You want my attention, you have to earn it."* The parent's attitude, all too often, is… *"Ok, as long as my child is happy."* I wanted teachers and presenters to realize that their obligation to their audience/class has dramatically shifted; from *getting* their attention to constantly having to *regain* their attention.

TEACHERS want to know: *"How do I get their attention?"* You must first accept that you can no longer do what you've always done… and expect to be successful. Accept, too, that the chemistry of the Group…*the make up of the individuals in your classroom or audience…* has dramatically and irreversibly changed. Their interest and attention in the topic, in the subject and in *you,* may differ dramatically from your own. Those of us who hope to remain presenters and teachers in the 21st century, must choose to adapt to a new audience…become immersed in technology… embrace our parents (the same way we would include our stakeholders in business)… love our audiences/children… and build rapport with our colleagues.

PARENTS *and TEACHERS* want to know: *"How can I get them to listen to me?"* Begin by admitting that you must take some ownership for the behaviors you have been teaching your children. Sometimes you are aware of the impact you have on your children… sometimes you aren't… sometimes you wish you weren't. The truth is, *they* are watching and learning from *you* ALL of the time. They watch your every move… from listening as you talk to and about others, to what you tell them *not* to do but do yourself. Remember, YOU are their first role model. They will follow *your* lead.

The first rule: *Say what you mean and mean what you say.* You must be consistent. If you said NO… and later relented to say YES… understand how this confuses the child. You *established* a boundary with your child, you *taught* that boundary to the child, and (at first) said NO when the child *pushed* that boundary. You then "gave in" to the pleas and tears and said YES. The child now recognizes that by pushing the boundary, it can be moved. The next time, on the same boundary, you say NO again and the child wonders how this could be: *"I thought it was now YES? I'm confused! If the boundary moved once, it can be moved again. Perhaps I just need to keep pushing until the boundary moves again."*

The second rule: *If you make a mistake with rule number one, don't pretend it didn't happen.* If you made a mistake, admit it. If you allowed a boundary to be stretched too far, and now see that as a mistake, don't make up excuses or stories to cover up why you did it (or keep doing it). As soon as possible, sit down with the child (or class) and "rebuild your boundaries." Until you do, the child knows that if the boundary can be so easily moved, even once, it can be moved even farther. Stop the confusion and conflict before it escalates. Sit down with the child and speak with – not *at* him/her—as this is the most direct way to rebuild broken boundaries. The good news: children understand honesty. The really good news: children are also forgiving. So whenever you recognize that boundaries have been exceeded (or simply do not exist), you can start over at any time by admitting to your mistake and explaining that the boundary needs to be reestablished. Be open, honest, and sincere. Both honesty and dishonesty must be taught; which do you want the child to learn?

Yes, like it or not, your children will grow to be independent individuals who will make independent decisions. Their decisions will be influenced by those they admire and respect, from the values they will pick up from television, the Internet, the children and adults at school, in the books they read, and on and on. But FIRST they will become products of the structure (boundaries) *you* taught them.

A Final Thought:

The next time you prepare to sit with a child or speak with a parent, or take your place before *the Group,* never doubt the fact that others want to be heard, too. They want to be entertained: they fear having to remember too much; they, too, hide behind masks; they *will* scrutinize your every word and action; and they *still* fully expect to walk away gratified (satisfied) and that *this* was *"worth my time."*

Recall the *best training* or staff development session *you* have ever experienced. Go ahead, think about it… I'll wait. If you liked it, you participated in it, which means you were involved, felt welcomed, and probably had interaction with your peers. What happened in that session to make that particular class, workshop, address or presentation stand out from other sessions you've attended?

√ Was it a warm, welcoming and relaxed setting for this session? When you walked into the room you knew in a flash whether or not this was a positive environment for this session, didn't you? The culture will literally set the stage in forming the attitude as to whether or not the listener wanted to be there.

√ Did the inflection of the presenter keep your interest? She (he) certainly did not speak in a monotone, speak too softly, or had an accent difficult to understand. Did the presenter fluctuate volume, punctuate main points, and use tone and inflection to maintain your interest?

√ Was it a presentation that incorporated all learning modalities: auditory, visual and hands-on (kinesthetic)? We are not, of course, one or the other, but aspects of each modality. By far, the vast majority of us, however, are kinesthetic and visual learners; we learn best in a class or presentation where we can *see and touch* the message. Statistically, only 1 in 12 of us is an auditory learner. Auditory learners accept information best if you could sit them in a corner and just "talk" to them. Note: If you are a classroom teacher, college professor, or presenter who just "lectures" *at* your students, this means that you are *knowingly* reaching only two of the 24 students in your class.

√ <u>Did the presenter show some personality</u>... some enthusiasm? Did she/he use gestures, facial expressions, move around the group, or otherwise demonstrate that he cared about the topic, about being there with you? Did the presenter send the message that the topic was important, and that she cared whether or not you... the listener... was *getting it*? Did she care about YOU?

√ <u>Was this staff development session interactive,</u> involving *the group* in technology, physical activities, demonstrations or in open exchanges with the presenter or others in the session?

√ <u>Did you smile, giggle and/or laugh out loud?</u> The adrenalin rush we know as laughter lifts the heart and opens the mind to a new way of learning. Where there is laughter, there is learning. We all differ in culture, background, learning styles, levels of education and life experiences. We learn best when we are enjoying ourselves (entertained and gratified). If you work to meet this Need for Fun in the Group (one of the five basic human Needs), providing some measure of joy in their day, you will have increased your groups' interest in *wanting* to listen.

√ <u>Was the presenter confident, knowledgeable and prepared?</u> If so, he/she was probably more concerned about his attitude toward the message he *had prepared*, as opposed to any audience attitudes, perceptions or judgments he could *imagine*. Confidence in yourself will always diminish your fears. You cannot be responsible for the imagination of others. You cannot *out think* whatever you imagine others *might* be thinking about you.

In this section we have examined some of the obstacles that inhibit listening: our Intrapersonal thoughts, in one-on-one exchanges, and how this influences the dynamics *of the individuals* in *the Group.* Now, let's go to the next section and find out what kind of listener YOU are. Determine for yourself if you are willing to become an Active Listener and how you can gain the attention and respect of your listeners.

Section 3

Are You Listening?

"Sometimes, without saying a word, you are speaking so loudly that I can't hear a thing you're saying!"

Chapters

    8. Hearing is *not* Listening!

    9. Words: Watts in a Word?

    10. Inflection: More important that the Truth of your message.

    11. Body Language:
        What you're saying....when you're saying Nothing at all!

    12. From Passive to Active … in 21 Days… Guaranteed!

Chapter 8

Hearing is Not Listening

"Listening is Love in Action."
—Scott Peck, ***The Road Less Traveled***

It happens thousands of times a day. It happens to you. You walk down the street or down the hall and notice someone coming your way. You look up in time to smile as he (she) makes this comment in passing: *"Hello, how are you?"* Not even slowing down, the one who asks continues on. You now wonder... does he really expect me to stop, turn around, smile, stare at his butt, wave, and answer with that compulsory: *"Fine, how are you?"*

Listening (to others or to your own self talk) requires no deliberate effort or action on your part. The brain requires no outside energy source (batteries included), and even the laziest among us can hear without exerting a modicum of energy. Hearing requires nothing on our part beyond the physical capacity to do so. It is Listening that takes effort.

For purposes of this book, let's say that... for the sake of brevity... the world is divided into three types of listeners: Non-listeners, Passive listeners, and Active listeners.

Many of us are **Non-listeners**:

A non-listener will do ALL the speaking (so he won't have to relate with you.)

He (she) has a "me first" attitude. He is too concerned with *me*, to leave any room for *you*.

You may get a few words in...but you will not be permitted to complete your thought, perhaps not even your sentence.

The agenda will remain with the non-listener.

He will send the distinct message, *"YOU are not important."*

He may be in front of you, but he will interrupt you to turn away to speak to others, wave or comment to those passing by, shake your hand but never look at you, and ask unrelated questions, all while pretending to be engaged with you. In the middle of your sentence he might ask, *"Do you know what time it is?"*

What does a Non-Listener "conversation" sound like? You get a phone call and the caller says, *"Hi, how are you?*

Your response is limited to, *"Hello."*

But without missing a beat, anticipating what he expected to hear, he has already moved on to what he is prepared to say, *"Fine, thank you."*

"I once got in line behind a salesman as he was greeting the receptionist behind the counter: *"Hi there,"* he said. *"How are you?"*

The response: *"Fine, thank you, how are you?"*

"Fine, thank you" he said, *"yourself?"*

"Good," the clerk continued, *"you doing all right?"*

"Yeah," he went on, *"doing ok, how are you?"*

"Good…Good."

The Non-listener is called a Non-listener because – duh, because he/she…doesn't!

Most of us are **Passive Listeners:**

A passive listener is non-threatening and non-judgmental. Her (or his) interest, however, is more in *having* an audience, than *being* an audience for you.

She will, however, allow you to speak and to complete entire sentences, even whole thoughts. But while you are speaking, she is formulating what *she* wants to say next.

You get the impression that while you are being treated politely, you are not really being heard. As a result, both of you will find yourselves…repeating yourselves.

Passive listeners will rob you of your focus, devaluing your concerns, ideas, and agenda by returning the focus to themselves.

Your *words* are being heard, but not necessarily the *intent* of what you are trying to express. The passive listener will interpret your words through her own experiences with little interest in looking beyond her own understanding to relate to you.

Little interest is also given to the intent of your inflection; even less attention to observing or reading your body language.

Passive learners steal the focus. They can often be heard to interrupt you with: *"You think THAT'S something, I remember the time when I…"*

Some of us are **Active Listeners:**

Being able to read the wants and discern the Needs others are trying to meet through their behaviors can best be accomplished through the form of communications known as Active Listening. This form of listening might best be described for what it is not: it is NOT moralizing, lecturing or offering unsolicited advice. It is listening completely with trust, honesty, and empathy. It is listening through observation and the awareness realized through Words, Inflection and Body Language.

Only 7-13% of what you understand from others comes through the <u>Words</u> they use; up to 37% of what you understand comes through <u>Inflection;</u> but as much as 80% of what you understand from others…and what they understand from you…comes through <u>Body Language</u> and other non-verbals. The best hope you have of truly understanding others…your family, coworkers and friends…will come through the application of all three of these forms of communications.

Follow me through these next several chapters on Words – Inflection – Body Language. If you want people to treat you differently, more positively, do it willingly, do it for life, you will choose to become…an ACTIVE LISTENER.

Chapter 9

Words: Watts in a Word?

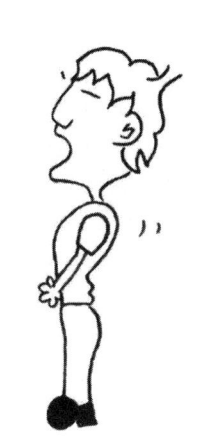

"I never said most of the things I said. I don't want to make the wrong mistake."

—Yogi Berra

You are able to read and make sense of what you are reading on these pages because you can associate these words with corresponding pictures you have formed in your head. If you have ever had a memory, you have "paper clipped" a word to the picture in your mind that describes that image. At the mere mention (or reading) of a single word, the files in your mind open, and an action is automatically triggered. For example:

Spaghetti...Disney...Reality TV...The Rodaca

In less than a heart beat, you "saw" a memory associated with each word. Here is how it works;

In the same way that a remote control changes images on your TV, or the click of your computer "mouse" will return an instant picture on your computer screen, the mention of a single word, as the examples above, will instantly open a file in your brain. As you read the four words above, a vision of an experience, the face of a person associated with the experience, a snapshot of something you witnessed, some memory...without your ability to control it...leaped into your mind. When you read The Rodaca, however, your brow wrinkled, you cocked your head slightly, and your eyes searched both the visual and auditory recall centers of the brain. Still, you received no "picture" to match the word. That is because there is no such word, so you had no experience to match to that label. No understanding, no label, no picture.

When your "hard drive" does not have that particular file in storage, try as you may, it would be impossible for your computer screen to reveal that which the hard drive does not possess. You may desperately want your computer to understand the command and to possess the file for which you seek, but if the information has not previously been "in-putted" (yeah, that's probably not a word...) then there is no way that information could later be accessed. There is no way to expect words like *The Rodaca* to register in the data base of your mind if it was never *entered*.

You are constantly seeking what you WANT in order to meet your inherent and persistent drive to meet your human Needs (see Behavior Cycle). To meet your Needs, you choose BEHAVIORS you believe will get you what you Want. The FEEDBACK you receive from your Behaviors tells you if you got what you wanted.

The CONSEQUENCE determines *what it costs*; was it "worth it" to get what you wanted. To get what you want, you must seek the cooperation of others. You will use **words** in your attempts to get others to understand what you want. You use *words* to meet your Needs. While words are the least effective form of communications, it is the form that receives the most attention, is the least credible for understanding, but carries the highest emotional impact.

Regardless of language, we place greater weight on the spoken word than all other forms of communications combined. Words have incredible power. As your daughter comes downstairs to meet her date for the prom, the nervous young man standing at the bottom of the stairs with mom, wanting to make a good impression, compliments his date. The words he uses may well establish just how pleasant the rest of the night is going to be. He says, *"You're cute."* (Cute? Do you think words like *pretty… beautiful…or gorgeous* would have been closer to the expectation? Could conflict begin with a compliment with something so well intended?)

Each description might be accurate, but which one would our prom princess (and mom) prefer to hear, or *expect* to hear? Which word would have had more of a positive impact with mom and daughter? Mom spent $80 on the hairdo, $700 on the gown, and $90 for shoes. The makeover, manicure, and the shopping for just the right handbag in anticipation of this very moment, certainly deserved more than *"You're cute."* Junior is off to a rocky start.

When words come to us, the mind requires no preparation to receive them. Words are nothing more than "labels" for the pictures in our mind. Once these words are delivered, without conscious thought, the mind races to match these labels to experiences in order to give context to the message. Instantly, the mind creates perceptions, finds amusement, places value, makes judgments, asks questions, and otherwise seeks further understanding to separate what was implied from what was heard or read. Yes, when we are not sure what is intended, we *imagine* we know what was meant, implied, offered, or inferred. We forget that communications (understanding) is not in the *intent* of the speaker, but in the message *received* by the listener.

The act of hearing words requires very little effort on our part. Perhaps it is for this very reason that we are so quick to assign meaning to the words we receive. We formulate judgments, leap to conclusions and break relationships based on a single comment or the utterance of a single word. Without further stimulus, a single word, in print or in expression, whether you want it to or not, will *instantly* conjure a mental picture and an understanding of what that word means to *you*. This may NOT necessarily have the same definition or intent for the speaker, but once defined by the *perception* of the listener, this single word can be perceived to mean whatever the listener's imagination wants to believe. *Words are labels for the pictures in our heads.*

For this reason, we labor over *just the right words* to say to comfort a friend at the loss of a loved one. We deliberate over what to say that will best convey our message in our professional correspondence, evaluations, greetings, prose, poetry, and more. We choose *just the right words* to seal the sale, encourage the disheartened, and correct the errant child. We express through *just the right words*, our emotions: our fears, love, anguish, disappointment, frustration, and excitement. And we are just as calculating in our selection of *just the right words* to reveal our distain, to threaten and intimidate, to deny our guilt or express our anger.

Words are important.

You drive down the street and see that two houses across the street from each other are having some home remodeling done. Each contractor has his sign posted proudly in his respective yard. In one yard the sign reads: "Craftsmen Builders." Across the street the sign reads, "Good Enough Construction." Which one strikes you as the builder you want working on your house?

Driving down Main Street through a small town in West Virginia, I glanced over to see this huge sign, in large letters, printed across the face of a building: "DROP YOUR PANTS HERE!" That struck me as odd; did I read that right? I couldn't turn around fast enough to see if I read that correctly. Sure, enough, what an interesting approach to get your customers attention...for a *dry cleaning* store.

Just a few years ago, if someone called you GAY, you accepted that as a compliment. You smile, someone takes your picture and this quote makes it to your local newspaper. You were being seen as content or happy. You, your family and co-workers couldn't wait to acknowledge the positive publicity. You would never envision how this could be considered a source of future conflict when, a few years later, you run for some local political office and someone quoted an old newspaper article that called you *GAY*. When that article was written, the word had an entirely new and different meaning. Could this be a source of conflict for this would-be politician?

Apply that same thinking to our understanding of something like... say... scripture. If the socially accepted understanding over a word like "GAY" could be so radically altered over the span of a decade, how might our perspective on the interpretation of words change over a couple of millennium?

When you read "fear God" in scripture, for example, what picture does your mind draw? With more and more violence and bullying reports in our schools, we say we "*fear* for the safety of our children." Just this moment I heard CNN report something about "...*fear* of future terror in the region." The word "fear" has more popularly come to mean to be afraid, or to be frightened. It is perfectly natural, therefore, to take this accepted meaning and apply it to every other usage of the word. Does "fear God" mean to be "afraid" of God? Would it help to understand the word *fear* if you knew how it was interpreted 2000 years ago? The word then took on a completely different understanding as *fear* was more closely defined as *respect*. Does *"respect God"* carry a different image for you than to *"be afraid of God?"*

In another scripture example, we read, *"What good would it do for a man to gain the whole world and lose his <u>soul</u> in the process?"* The more commonly accepted image of *soul* today comes from the Greek and conjures up pictures more synonymous with invisible spirits—that part of us that leaves us in death and goes to heaven. Another interpretation comes from the Hebrew culture, from the region where this sentence originated; where this understanding would be more closely associated with another word we are familiar with: *personality*. Would this change your understanding? Would how you interpret a single word determine how you would interpret the entire message?

Let's say your parents wanted you to be a doctor. Your parents were doctors, their parents were doctors, and your older sibling was a doctor, now you are expected to be a doctor, too. You may have wanted to be an architect, but you felt the pressure, the obligation of family to be a doctor. Begrudgingly, for the love and concern you had for your family, you feel obligated to become a doctor. So you worked and sacrificed to become a doctor. Your heart still pulls you to being an architect, but you are now a doctor. You have money, power, and even fame…but you are unhappy, moody, and still long for a different life because you have not yet fulfilled your own dream. If you use the latter understanding of the word soul to mean *personality,* now reword the question: *"What good would it be for a man to gain the whole world and lose his <u>personality</u> in the process?"* Would that perspective alter your understanding?

It is said that a picture is worth a thousand words, so we try to paint pictures with our words to help describe the images we see. Think of the analogies you use. Analogies are not "truth" and they obviously aren't intended to be "accurate" depictions. They are broad stroke impressions that "paint" instant images. For example:

> Compared to steel, aluminum is "light as a feather."
> The diet must be working—Mary is as "thin as a rail."
> The dog that jumped out in front of me was as "big as a house!"
> Your honor, my client was not "high as a kite."
> Billy is a smart boy; he is as "sharp as a tack."
> I had the flu and was as "sick as a dog."

How does the marketing profession use words? In your local stores, for example, advertisers essentially have only shape, color and *words* to describe the products that line their shelves. How are they attempting to alter your shopping habits with just their *words*?

Designer jeans: This means that for an extra fifty dollars, you can be "in fashion" and have a special patch on your butt. You are now wearing *designer* jeans.

The *Giant Economy Size*: It doesn't matter that two regular size boxes might contain more product for less price; the Giant Economy Size *sounds* like a bargain!

New *and Improved:* It's new *and* improved! Wow, what a deal; not only *new*, but *improved*, too. How can I pass that up? And it's on sale!

Foods for good health: How many brands or catch phrases can you name that speak to clean living and long life? *Healthy Choice – FAT free – low fat – 20% less fat – Reduced fat – No Tran fats – Low in Calories high in Energy – Nature's own – High fiber and low in cholesterol –* and on and on. Thank goodness, I won't have to exercise; I know I can depend on this product because now I *believe* I'll be eating better. I feel better already!

Grey Poupon: One of my personal favorites. Be like the rich and famous. Use this product and you, too, may be chauffeured in a Rolls Royce. It sounds rich and classy...but it's just MUSTARD.

You have heard that beauty is in the *eye* of the beholder. It is equally true that words are interpreted in the *mind's eye* of the beholder. Throughout the world, people of like ethnicity...race, religions, values, beliefs and interests...form informal and formal cultural communities. They share a like-mind; we seek out like-minded people. We base our relationships on such things; we like people who are *like us*...people to whom we can relate. Conversely, we tend to distrust or dislike people who do not agree with us; people to whom we *cannot* relate. *"Hey, I was thinking the same thing!"* or *"I was just going to say that."* Such declarations put the "relate" into "relationship."

Within each culture, within each community, within each family, understanding is dependent upon our ability to *relate* to others. We use language and the use of universal or commonly understood words as a foundation for the building of relationships. Understanding depends on more than how each *speaker* interprets the words within that particular culture. All cultures, formal and informal...clubs, professions, organizations...have their own language, buzz words, acronyms and slang. Understanding and rapport comes out of the experiences and expectations of the *listener;* from how the *listener* interprets the words of the speaker. Even though all within the culture are aware that words hold multiple meanings, those unfamiliar with that culture have no other framework for understandings beyond their *own* culture or life experiences. Do you understand the language from these cultures?

"You dig the kicks?"　(You like my shoes?)
"I just got knocked up."　(In Australia, you just got a pay raise)
"He's a happy pappy."　(In Appalachia, dad got his welfare check)
"The fox is da bomb dog."　(A fox is a pretty lady; da bomb means great performance; dog? Ask Randy Jackson.)

While words cannot convey *intent*, intent is often assumed from our words. Words do not convey understanding, yet understanding is assumed from our Words. The difference between *understanding* and *intent* is referred to as *perception*. The most common pathway to human Interpersonal conflict comes not from the intent, but from the perceptions that are taken from the words that we say, read, hear and *imagine*. Everyone has different experiences so everyone will have a slightly different perspective or slant on the words used to describe and interpret those experiences. Conflict is inherent to the nature of words because the best of intentions are no match for individual perceptions.

When one person's "all I know and understand" world is exposed to thinking that is completely foreign to what was previously known, accepted, valued or believed, conflict *will* surface. Our inability to accept each other's differences, the differences between what we know and what we perceive, breeds misunderstandings and conflict. The gap in our experiences represents the vast differences in our understanding of what we *think* other people should or ought to do, or say, or know in virtually any situation. In order to communicate with another you need to begin on common ground.

A Proverb from Hebrews says: *"Do not confine your children to your own learning, for they were born in a different time."* For those of us who are grandparents, let's go back to "the 60's" for a minute. What an emotionally charged period this was. If you lived it, it became a part of you. Many struggled with Vietnam as flower children, pacifists, protesters, or combatants. We were getting used to the word "Sputnik" as man raced to build the first rocket to the moon. On the evening news, we watched intently to learn how close our country was to destruction as we watched two nuclear powers in a confrontation at sea we would later call the Cuban Missile Crisis. If you were alive, you vividly remember President Kennedy's assassination. It is not something we had to learn in a history book; to us, these were our current events, providing vivid and emotional memories.

Those of us who lived during the 60's, therefore, naturally possess experiences and a vocabulary of related terms that carry emotional weight. These experiences would be far removed from our children's and grandchildren's experiences. The same can be said for the 70's, 80's, 90's and so on: if you lived it, you could readily relate to it. Each individual's ability to relate to others comes from the emotions, perceptions and understanding each derives from his or her own experiences. The independent experiences of every parent, teacher, and child will naturally be what each uses to communicate, what each will use to establish common ground.

Adults and children live in a completely different *"all I know and understand world."* Our inability to relate to each other, however, is *not* because we have vastly different experiences. Our conflict rages on because of our unwillingness to *accept* that others are *"different from me."* The strength of a single word could end a relationship if the feelings, perceptions and experiences of others are ignored or not taken into consideration. Communications begins on common ground. To get to common ground, everyone must be *willing* to move from where they are, to find common *understanding*.

At home, our experience gap might look something like this: Let's say mom and her teen stand in the doorway of your child's bedroom, and the unkempt sight of what lies within sparks this brief exchange of words:

"Ain't my *crib cool*?"
"Your what?"
"My *digs, man,* you know, my room?
"I'm your mother, not *man*, and the temperature of the room young man is not in question here."
"*Chill* mom, it's *neat*."
"This is a mess, it is certainly far from *neat*?"
"*Get down,* mom!
"The only thing down, young man, is you on the floor cleaning this up."

In school, when students do not as yet have the level of understanding that the teacher expects them to have, the teacher might say, *"You ought to know better."* or *"You should know this by now."* Rather than instruct the child, the teacher chooses only to condemn the child. With such statements, the implication that the child is not smart enough to be at this grade level is not missed by the child. Words like *stupid or dummy* come to mind and children already place far too much value on the meanings of words at this age. He understands these words; he is not yet as experienced as the teacher at finding *excuses* rather than *solutions*.

As a teacher or parent, young and impressionable children already think that you know everything! They look up to you. They would rather pass out than say this out loud, of course, but in truth, parents and teachers, YOU are their role models. They trust your wisdom, advice, understanding, and counsel. They compare themselves to you…every moment of every day, whether you want them to or not. Because you appear more knowledgeable, they see you to be "smarter" then they are. When you send the message to children (in word, inflection or body language), that they are not measuring up to your expectations, not good enough, not smart enough, do not behave like they "should," don't perform well enough in school, or don't excel in sports, they clip words like "stupid" and "dummy" to their mental pictures of self worth. What if we could begin viewing each other as having differing levels of *experience* rather than one of us having to be *smarter* than the other?

In fact, we teachers and parents may not be smarter than our children at all; we *are* more experienced. As every experience results in a memory, it is only natural that adults would have many more memories than their children. As a result, adults have many, MANY more words in their vocabulary, the capacity to make inferences and the applications associated to the multiple meanings of the words, and to make greater implications and imagery for the experiences they have gathered over the many years of their lives.

73

Every experience also comes with a consequence. As we grow older, we become more aware of these consequences, measured against every decision to determine if the behaviors we have chosen in life were worth the cost. As we come to accept the expectation that we will be held accountable for the consequences of our actions, we grow in understanding; in the intangible complexity derived of human behavior known as *maturity*.

We adults have an edge over our children as experience allows us to look backwards to assess the potential for conflict in the future. Children have not yet developed the level of experience, maturity or wisdom from past consequences to look very far backwards. Children, obviously, have not lived long enough to make all the blunders we have. While we can intellectually understand that, we continue to provide such profound instructions to our children as, *"don't touch this,"* or *"don't play with that,"* and *"don't lick the gum blobs stuck on the seat."* When they do it anyway (and they *will* do it anyway), rather than attempt to help draw mental pictures for them as to *why* such interesting challenges might be unhealthy or unsafe, we often launch into our *"you should know better"* mode. *You* learned by experience, yet you want them to just *"know better"* because *you* know better? They "should know better" … why? Did you teach the understanding… or just hope for it?

A sixth grade girl entered an Internet chat room and began conversing with "a friend." Sure, her teachers and parents *told* her not to, but it was fun and what could it hurt? Mom knew her daughter was spending too much time on "*that d— computer.*" She became suspicious only after she noticed a change in her daughter's attitude and even in her vocabulary. Mother didn't want to say anything, however, because "*I knew it would cause an argument."* Mom didn't want to risk "*making her daughter mad.*"

Mother, of course, remembers distinctly *telling* her daughter that she "*should not*" get in those chat rooms so mom couldn't understand how "*things got out of hand.*" Wherever mom drew her own imagery, she held clear pictures in her mind to match the warning labels she placed on such words as *"child porn, manipulation, rape"* and much worse. Mother "knew better" but chose "keeping her happy" because, "*she wanted to be her daughter's friend"* rather than her mother.

The ensuing conflict was inevitable. Her daughter, seeing the world from a lifetime of being protected and shielded from consequence, believed the world would always be all warm and fuzzy. Within the first two lines in the exchange between mom and child, mom will have it all neatly framed for her when the daughter cries, *"You don't understand (me)!"* The daughter, functioning out of her Need for Love and Acceptance, simply wanted to impress this "new guy" she met on line. Mom's fear is associated with her understanding; an understanding based on life experiences that her daughter didn't have. Without being taught such an understanding, her daughter had no fear.

An Aside: Just *telling* rather than *teaching* her daughter that she "should not" get on-line, had about as much impact on the prevention of this crime as that multi-million dollar ad campaign to stop drug abuse: *"Just say NO to drugs."* If you want something understood… TEACH it… don't hope for it!

We tend to assume our children "ought to" have the same level of understanding we do and that they "should" behave the way we want them to. As adults, as their parents and teachers, we take our own self-assured pictures of how the world "ought to be" and try to <u>will</u> that vision of the world into our children. The problem we seem to have difficulty grasping, is that children don't understand the world as we do; they can not yet *see* what we *see*. Children don't even understand all the words we're using in trying to describe it.

Children, without the conscious understanding of the many nuances of voice inflection and body language, are only "works in progress." As a result, children are so much easier to read than adults, relying primarily on words and emotions to convey their wants and concerns. When you speak, therefore, out of *your world of experience*, be aware of the child's blank expression that is telling you that this word or expression is not yet in her/his world of understanding. Instead of assuming knowledge, what an opportunity this is to *teach* the child new memories, new knowledge, new WORDS to build that data base of experiences.

A parent makes every attempt to teach his/her child honesty, integrity, and tact. In front of Aunt Sadie, the parent says to the child, *"You should smile and say thank you to Auntie for the gift."* When Aunt Sadie leaves, the child overhears Dad saying to Mom, *"That sure was an ugly gift from Aunt Sadie."* Later that night the parent says to the child; *"I know you didn't like it, but you should have told her that you DID like it."* In the morning he says: *"We'll take Aunt Sadie's gift back to the store but we can't tell her."*

Do you think the child got the message? What message is that?

Did the child understand the *words* of the parent? Probably.

Did the child understand the *intent* of the parent? Not sure.

Is it more likely that the parent just *assumed* understanding not yet apparent to the inexperienced mind of the child? "Should" the child understand merely because the *parent* understood what he meant?

As children move through puberty and adolescence, they learn from us to communicate with more than just words to get what they want. They learn how to consciously incorporate inflection and body language as well. Adults have become proficient at concealing their emotions and intent. Children learn from adults. As they grow into adulthood, they become more and more comfortable with the masks we taught them to wear. We taught them to be polite when they would rather fume and feign acceptance when their hearts are broken. We also taught them to Control to get what they want. Children must be *taught* to be deceitful.

An Aside: Children are intelligent; they want to learn. They are watching and listening *all of the time.* If you are not consistent with your words and your actions, you are still teaching and they are still learning…even if it is not the lesson you intended.

A Final Thought

I am a fisherman. If I have a lure in my tackle box that I know only works 7% to 13% of the time, I realize before I toss that lure into the water that I'm going to have only marginal success if I use that lure all by itself. To increase my chances of connecting with a fish, I am going to have to combine one method of catching fish, with other approaches as well. In the same way, to effectively communicate, I will have to add "just the right words" with inflection and body language to increase my chances of connecting with others. My goal in relationship building…my role as an active listener… is to relate to my speaker, to enter the world of others. I can only do that when I am not limiting myself to just Words.

In my very first year in education (nearly 4 decades ago), I was teaching a science unit on ocean life to seventh graders. Two students at a table in the back of the room wouldn't stop whispering to each other. When I couldn't avoid it any longer, I stopped the lesson and offered this challenge to my distracters. In my very best teacher voice, I said, *"Ok, whatever it is you two are talking about, I'm sure it's important enough to share with the entire class."* Feeling oh, so in charge now, I said, *"So, tell us what you're talking about."*

Without the slightest hesitation and with a sincere desire to respond to what she deemed was a sincere request, Mary looked up at me and asked, *"Well, Billy and I were just wondering, how many testicles does an octopus have?"*

Before I could lift my jaw off the floor, in that moment between the tenuous control I had over 30 seventh graders, and losing it completely, Mary saved me, *"Well, Billy says it has eight legs, and I think it has six."*

I managed to say, *"Why don't you look it up and tell us tomorrow."* I went on with the lesson.

Chapter 10

Inflection: More Important Than the Truth of Your Message

"When attempting to motivate, no word can be more powerful than the delivery."
—Coach Vince Lombardi

My favorite story of inflection comes from the popular radio talk show host, Paul Harvey. During the hectic shopping season before Christmas, a shopper, loaded down with packages, was walking through the parking garage in search of her car. When her car was in sight, she took only a few more steps before realizing that there were four teenage boys sitting inside. Stunned, she shouted, *"Hey, get out of that car."* Apparently unphased by this woman, the boys did not even acknowledge her presence.

Now becoming angry, she took another step forward and yelled: *"I said, get out of the car!"*

The boys now turned in her direction. But rather than leaving the car, they began laughing at her.

Now determined, she took yet another step towards the car, dropped her packages, pulled a revolver out of her purse, leveled it at the car and screamed, "I *SAID*, GET OUT OF THE CAR!"

The smiles dropped from the faces of the four boys. Instantly, all four doors flew open and all four boys flew out of the car and took off in four different directions.

The lady was feeling so proud of herself now. A moment later, however, she looked over this now empty car and saw *her* car parked...three spaces down.

In the same way that words are nothing more than labels for the pictures in your head, you use voice inflection and tone to provide *texture,* that which injects *feeling* into those mental pictures. You choose just the right "label" to use with voice inflection when you want to more effectively communicate your messages. The label itself, remember, is sufficient to provide understanding between 7-13% of the time. The use of inflection will increase understanding as much as 37% of the time.

Inflection is not only important to effective communication, inflection is often perceived to be *more important* than the truth of your message. The meaning of words now shifts to where you place the emphasis.

<u>She's</u> dead.
She's <u>dead.</u>
<u>She's</u> dead?
She's <u>dead</u>?
She's <u>dead!</u>

When the minister suddenly gestures and raises his voice to make a point, your mind jumps to attention and says, *"Pay attention to this…this must be important or he wouldn't have shouted it!"* Until that moment, were your thoughts drifting? Did this sudden change of inflection "bring you back?"

The teacher says, *"Ok, now what does **THAT** have to do with the answer to this **NEXT** question?"* A moment ago, that book you had not found much interest in, now takes on the importance of the Bible: *"You can see I'm intently reading here, teacher, so don't direct that question to me."*

Let me ask you this question: *"How many animals of each **SPECIES** did Moses take aboard the ark?"* In that example, your brain went on hold for a split second while you "looked up" the inflected word. You did that automatically; that is, you heard the stressed word and sought meaning to it before the rest of the sentence was spoken. You did it without conscious thought because you heard your brain say, *"Hmmm, the speaker wouldn't have stressed it if it wasn't important."* As you found meaning to the inflected word, you may have completely missed the rest of the sentence…and the truth of the message…as it was Noah, not Moses, who made that trip.

Inflection can bring your awareness back to the present or divert your attention from the subject at hand. When the parent scolds the child about the merits of keeping a clean bedroom, she might say, *"This room is **ALWAYS** a mess."* The child immediately focused on the inflected word and takes offense because she remembers that three weeks ago Tuesday she did clear a spot around the make-up table. What would follow would be an argument over the last time it was cleaned rather than the intent of the message; that the room needed to be cleaned…again.

Sometimes inflection can be conspicuous by its absence. I recall a television commercial that opened with a mother on the phone talking to her son in college. The point of the commercial was to demonstrate how clearly you could hear if you used this particular phone company. Mom would ask, *"How are you doing, Johnny?"* The boy would respond, *"Fine."* He would then say, *"Hey, is that Dad coming home from work?"*

Mom would say, *"Yes, that's Dad; but how are <u>you</u>, Johnny?"* Again, Johnny would say, *"I'm fine, Mom."* He then adds, *"Is that Bobby opening the refrigerator* *door?"* After mom responded, Johnny again asked if that was brother Billy bouncing a basketball through the kitchen. Mom would say, *"Yes, that is Billy, but, Johnny, how are YOU?*

Her next line had a much deeper message than the clarity of the phone line: *"Johnny, how are you...really? I can hear, too, you know."* What mom could "hear" was the *absence* of feeling.

When I was in the seminary, I remember going into the lounge area where one of my teachers, Sister Judith, was sitting alone. She smiled, she asked about my day, we chatted, I laughed, told her a story or two, and was enjoying our conversation. Perhaps ten minutes later another seminary student walked in, sat down, and joined in our discussion. Within thirty seconds, my classmate lowered his voice, looked at Judith and asked: *"Do you want to talk about it?"*

Her eyes almost immediately welled up with tears. She began to share what had apparently been bothering her all day...and I completely missed it. It wasn't in her expression or her words; it was the *absence* of inflection that I missed. I was too wrapped up in my own day, my own concerns, my own Needs to catch what I would later look back on as obvious signs of her distress. I had missed something that wasn't there... yet discernable for that very reason... because of what was *not* there. As we all have pivotal moments in our lives, that was one moment, one lesson, I would never forget.

A Final Thought:

Several years ago, a lady and her daughter came up to me after a conference where we had been discussing personality profiles, our human Needs, and how to build more positive relationships between parents and teens. The mother and daughter had apparently been discussing their differences. The mother looked at her daughter and said, *"Go ahead; ask him."* Reluctantly, the daughter asked, *"If someone uses very little tone or voice inflection, does this mean that this person has a negative attitude?"* Wow, I wondered, where did that come from? My answer, of course, was, *"No, not at all."*

Mother was apparently trying to find a label for her daughter, so she tried again. This time, asking in the first person, she wanted to know, *"Well, how can I tell if I am a pessimist or an optimist?"* Without thinking (I do this whenever I want to place my foot in my mouth), I told her the answer to that question is always revealed by the first words she speaks every morning. They both cocked their heads and looked puzzled.

I looked to the left and then to the right...then I whispered, as if only these two should hear this "secret." With a straight face and a calm, even voice, I began, *"When you get up tomorrow morning, your first words will determine if you are an optimist or a pessimist. Which will you say? <u>GOOD morning, God!</u> or <u>Good God, it's morning</u>."*

Chapter 11

Body Language and other *Non*-verbals: What you're saying when you're saying nothing at all!

"Kindness is the only language the deaf can hear and the blind can see!"
—Mark Twain

    I was standing at a bus stop waiting with a few other folks for our ride. Standing behind me was a young married couple having what my mother would have called, "a tiff." They were debating some of the virtues of married life and a difference of opinion that will naturally arise in such unions. They apparently didn't care who was listening, and the three of us standing in front of them did not turn around. Suddenly the discussion behind ended as the "she" in the conversation waited for a reply from her mate. The three of us who were pretending not to hear, laughed out loud when the next voice we heard was one of female indignation as she demanded, *"Don't look at me with that tone of voice!"*

    We have established that *words* are nothing more than labels or name tags for our experiences: the unseen pictures in our minds. *Inflection* gives texture…providing both feeling and perspective to those pictures; but it is *body language* that inserts the action into our pictures, bringing out into the open that which has remained unspoken. Body language gives form…viable, almost tangible *substance* to these images.

    Hearing the action of words, feeling the intent, and reading body language and other non-verbal cues are essentials in the establishment of highly effective communication skills. This is the pathway to enter the world of others. We do this *not* with an eye *to judge* others. The intent in focusing on words, inflection, and body language cues is to better empathize, understand, relate to, and accept those who have simply asked us to *"Please listen to me."* Ultimately, our objective is to assist others in the resolution of their Intrapersonal confusion and their Interpersonal conflicts.

Your goals in communications are to convey your mental pictures, the events and emotions, in the most effective way possible; to ensure that others are seeing (understanding) what your minds eye sees; to assist others in their understanding; and to establish rapport. Words convey a small percentage of understanding; inflection can convey even more. But as much as 50—80% of what others will understand about you will be revealed through body language and other non-verbals.

The fictional character of Sherlock Holmes, Conan Doyle's character adaptation of his real life college professor Dr. Joseph Bell, is best known for his astounding powers of observation. By your gate, what you wear, your accent, your features, your mannerisms, etc, our hero Sherlock could deduce much about an individual. These words from Dr. Bell are what inspired Conan Doyle to write this popular series: *"Because we hear, we see but we do not observe. Because we do not observe, we see one to be no different than another. Because we see one to be no different than another, we see others to be no different from ourselves. We see others, only as we see ourselves."* Sherlock was unique because he "listened" through observation. *"When listening to what one sees,"* he noted, *"the body can not lie."*

Body communications and other non-verbal cues are extensive. The number of books on such topics could fill a small library. As it applies to the intent of this book, however, to promote bonding relationships through active listening, we are going to limit our discussion to becoming *familiar* with Body Language. The intent is to help you leap from a world where you have been conditioned to listening only with your ears… to accepting that there is an entire world of listening through observation. And *that* world, you may find, is an entire universe beyond the world to which you may have been accustomed.

In this discussion we can loosely lump body language and non-verbals under five broad headings: Facial Expressions, Gestures, Movement Messages, Eyes, and Silence.

Facial Expressions

Facial expressions are referred to as the "mood" barometer. When you stand in front of your bathroom mirror, you may glance at your body to make sure your outfit isn't wrinkled or your tie is straight, but your focus is above your neck. Make-up application, drying and combing hair, checking for bags under those eyes, observing your smile, frowning, turning your head side to side, looking up and down to check out *the look* and otherwise making sure the look you *are* projecting matches the look you are *intending* to project.

As a school principal in a rural school, the faculty and I always worked to promote a positive culture where students could readily relate with staff, where school-community relationships were important, and where a positive school climate could reduce Interpersonal conflicts. A clearly understood structure existed within the school, communications were open, and boundaries were clear and well established in the classrooms. The attitude of the staff and students, therefore, was generally upbeat and the relationships with students and parents were courteous, warm, and friendly. That is probably why this next story always brings a smile.

I remember sitting at my desk when a teacher came charging through my office door holding a boy in one hand and a note in the other. He put the note on my desk and held the boy out in front of him. The boy had been on the receiving end of a note passed in class. The boy look shocked and the red-faced teacher looked like he would explode: *"Read the note!"* he demanded. This is the same teacher that has a sign over his door that says, "SMILE… CHOOSE to be HAPPY!"

I couldn't imagine what could evoke such anger in this otherwise calm and fun loving teacher. As I unfolded the note, I expected the worst. As I finished reading the words on the page, I deliberately bit the side of my cheek until I could regain my composure. The note that apparently struck a nerve with this teacher had read: *"If Mr. Jones is so damn happy, I wish he would notify his face!"*

On another occasion, I was conducting a seminar on body language and had two people on stage to do a demonstration. While they were role playing, I stepped to the end of the stage and waited. I glanced down to the front row and saw a couple smiling while she poked her mate and repeated, *"Ok, I get… I get it."* When the demonstration was over, I told the young couple that caught my attention that I was curious. I asked her what she meant when she kept saying, *"I get it."* She smiled again and said, *"I really do get it now. I know what he means now when he says, 'Don't yell at me with your face!'"*

Gestures

Sigmund Freud said *"Gestures are nature's way of purging the truth."* At a conscious level, we attempt to conceal the truth behind the masks that we wear—the masks we use to protect our fragile egos from a critical and judgmental world. Freud said, *"The conscious mind can be likened to a water fountain."* He said the *subconscious* mind was *"a veritable ocean from which the fountain draws."* Experience (memories) are not lost, only stored in the expanse of this "ocean" and available for immediate recall. Trying to conceal the truth indefinitely, therefore, would be impossible; it would be like trying to indefinitely hold wood under water.

The more the mind attempts to *consciously* suppress what lies just below the surface… like trying to hold wood underwater… the more likely it is that the *subconscious mind* will release the "truth" to be revealed. The truth will always be just beneath the waves and will "surface" through the body in times of stress.

When former President Clinton was asked at a press conference if he ever had sex with his former intern, a defensive Bill Clinton stood at the lectern and said, *"I did not have sexual relations with that woman, Ms. Lewinsky."* While his words and inflection said "NO," his attempts to hold back the truth… in the biting of his lower lip, his blinking eyes and the noticeable nodding of the head… all were screaming "YES."

The raising of the voice, the aggressive tone, and posturing to keep people from asking further questions, and turning away from the podium immediately *after* the denial were all indicative of subconscious, desperate attempts to keep the truth concealed. Even answering the question by *repeating* the question *before the denial* is indicative of a lie: "No, I *did not* have sex with that woman, Ms. Lewinsky." You cannot indefinitely hold wood underwater, nor can you forever prevent the truth from surfacing. As Freud said, *"Gestures are nature's way of purging the truth."*

Jean Auel's first book, *Clan of the Cave Bear,* told the story of a tribe of men and women at the dawn of humanity, a time before the clan had the capacity to speak. Finding a young white girl lost from a far different tribe than their own, they took her in to raise her as one of their clan. This girl's tribe had evolved much farther than their own as this girl had the capacity to speak. They could not speak so they were not conditioned to *listening* with their ears. Because she could speak and had learned to interpret the intentions of others through her tribe's words, she made an astute observation: *"Because these people could not speak… they could not lie."*

Are YOU telling the truth? Here are some other examples as to how body language might reveal a discrepancy between *what you say and what you mean*.

An inconsistency or pause between a smile and a statement. That is, when one would follow the other rather than at the same time: *"You look really attractive tonight."* The smile might follow the statement instead of the smile being *a part of* the statement… as if the action followed the event rather than flowing together in a sincere expression.

When the boss folds his (her) arms and/or crosses his legs, we recognize that as "being closed." When used as gestures, the same is true. When the body disagrees with what the words are saying, the speaker's gestures and motions will remain noticeably closer to his own body. This is an attempt to avoid revealing what is behind the mask. This is contradictory to the more open and expressive gestures to be expected when there is nothing the subconscious mind is trying to conceal.

The eyes are considered the 'gateway to the soul.' Be wary when he looks away rather than holding the level of eye contact that would be consistent for this individual. Eye contact is difficult while trying to conceal the truth.

Withholding "frontal" posture is another indicator: turning the head or body away, walking away, and then suddenly returning that gaze or posture. These are independent acts spawned by independent thoughts…not congruent actions associated with a truthful response.

Putting the hand over the mouth when speaking…as if to hold back a lie.

Watch for the touching or itching of the nose, scratching behind the ears, or repeatedly blinking. Watch for it when your boyfriend explains, *"I had to work late."*

Notice when someone immediately becomes defensive when asked a direct question. This is not to be confused with someone who goes on the *offensive*. A strong desire to defend one's actions is a clear red flag that there is something just below the surface.

If sitting, watch the hands. Notice the rubbing of the hands together, moisture on the hands (or brow), distracting motions with the hands, or absent mindedly fondling objects in front of him. While focusing on the story he is telling, he may be placing or moving objects on the table as if he is placing an invisible barrier between you and him…as if building a wall he hopes you can't see around.

Other gestures send different messages:
Signs of *"I am superior to you"* include touching the tips of the fingers together, feet up on the desk, the arms/hands behind the head, and standing while you sit. Even when these are unrealized by the one sending the signals, the one receiving the signals often gets that message.

You briefly visit a friend in the hospital. You stop by and visit twice in two days. On the first visit, you sat in the chair and stayed 10 minutes. On the second visit, you stood up for 5 minutes. Because standing will place the patient in an inferior, uncomfortable position, the patient will invariably say the longer visit was when you stood beside him. Standing is a superior position; sitting implies that we are equals.

When the teacher in the classroom stands over a child, the message is *"I'm superior to you."* It may not be the intended message, but when that teacher bends over or drops to a knee beside the child's desk, there is a world of difference in how the student receives that attention. When the teacher calls the student to her/his desk, the child and teacher are no longer superior or inferior to each other, they are now, literally, *'on the same level.'*

A close friend loses a loved one so you go to the home to show your respects. You don't want to go, of course, for the same reason most people don't want to go; *"because I don't know what to say."* You feel obligated to go, to console your friend, but you don't want to embarrass yourself so you really do stress over, *"What do I say?"*

An Aside: We somehow still believe, even in times like these, that life is *"all about me."* Do you believe you are so important that others actually expect you to take away their pain? Do you believe it is your place, or your responsibility to make it all better? If you can't fix this (and you know you can't), then your immediate objection for not wanting to go is, *"I don't know what to say."* It sounds like YOU are the one needing to be consoled.

Surely it has occurred to you that there is nothing you can possibly say that would fill the hole in your friend's heart left by this loss. Oddly enough, it is not your words that your friend needs or wants right now. That which would be most heartfelt and welcomed is your presence; perhaps a hug, her hand in yours, or a touch on the shoulder to let her know that you are there for her. In *this* will be *your* comfort. Wait for it, your confirmation will be the smile, the returned hug, shared tears, a gentle squeeze of your hand, and the profound knowledge that your friend *"will not have to endure this moment... alone."* Your willingness to be present for your friend is the gift you offer... not your words.

When the teacher walks around the room, a simple and apparently off-handed gesture to place a hand on the shoulder of a student is a powerful statement to the child. The wise teacher recognizes when a child is having a bad day, feels the pressure of being unaccepted from his/her peers, just made a poor grade, needs a role model, has a rough home life or just needs a sign of adult acceptance. That same teacher understands that in the two seconds it took to touch that child's shoulder, that child was just elevated in status before his/her peers. For in that moment, everyone in that class recognized that *"I came into relationship with the TEACHER!"* This is when the superior (standing) position of the teacher can be channeled; lifting the spirits of those who, for whatever reason, find themselves feeling inferior to others.

Gestures, of course, like all body communications, offer our best attempts to describe the pictures in our head. *You* can see the picture in your head, so with words, inflection and gestures, you do your level best to bring those pictures to life... so *other* people can see what you see. This is, after all, the goal of communications.

My wife and best friend for over 40 years, the Teacher Down the Hall who inspired this seminar series and all these books, is a full-blooded Italian. Her parents came over on the boat from the old country. Italians, as you are aware, are very expressive. Irene uses gestures even if she is telling you what time it is. Now here is a girl that could not lie. At a party one time, our friends were teasing her about how animated she is. They told her that without gestures, she probably couldn't say a thing. We laughed because even as she was saying "No," those hands and arms were waving. Just for fun, we asked her to sit down... with her hands under her... so she couldn't use her arms. What a great sport! She sat down and started to say something, stopped, repeated herself, stopped again, her head and upper body swaying back and forth and... it was true: she couldn't speak a lick! Gestures: They are nature's way.

Movement Messages

When our children were small, they played with little toys that were called *Action Figures*. These toys were "brought to life" by moving their body parts. Another common way to read non-verbal body communications occurs when we add motion or action to our gestures. These are referred to as Movement Messages.

When the politician raises his voice, or pounds the podium, he is trying to get your attention so he can make his point.

What message did you get when your boyfriend wanted to say goodnight on your porch after that first date? He was fumbling with the change in his pocket, leaning awkwardly against the railing, or tripping over his words. He wanted to send a message that said *"No, I'm not nervous."* His words were saying *"No"* but his body language was screaming, *"HELP ME!"*

Your friend is walking slowly, head down, arms folded or behind her... as if she is *carrying the weight of the world on her shoulders*.

You notice a coworker repeatedly wringing his hands or rubbing his hands up and down on his arms... as if he was *trying to rub the worry, fear, pain, etc., out of him*.

Motions and gestures are powerful non-verbal cues. I used these and other non-verbals in my work as a university administrator when one of my responsibilities was to supervise 28 employees. In my office, my desk was across the room from the doorway and turned to face the wall so as not to represent a barrier. My chair could easily turn to face the door if someone entered.

In the corner of the room was a small end table with two identical chairs, one on either side. When an employee came in and wanted to talk, either professionally or socially, we each sat in one of these chairs as professional peers. My desk chair was intentionally raised (superior position) so it could be recognized as an elevated position from the other seats in the room. When an employee needed to be reminded of policy or procedures, I sat facing them in my desk chair...as the boss...and the employee sat in his chair. When the issue was more severe, and the employee required consequences for his actions, I stood and the employee sat. I once had an employee who seriously jeopardized his job, so I put him in my seat and I sat in his and asked, *"What would you do if you were me?"*

He fired himself.

Eye Contact

We all come from differing worlds of experience. To relate to another, you must be willing to enter the world of experience that others live in. To enter that world, you must be willing to "read" or recognize the cues. You can, almost literally, enter the mind of another by entering that world through their eyes. The eyes are one of the most powerful non-verbal cues you possess. If you don't believe that, scoot up close to your significant other, look directly into his eyes, and whisper *"Do you love me?"* Watch the eyes. Are his eyes dilating slightly? If so, the answer is definitely, YES! (This only works on males.)

Do you play poker? If the guy across from you is raising his bet... and his eyes are dilating... he is not bluffing.

Your eyes can even determine if you are speaking the truth.

Since it is not practical to watch your own eyes, watch the eyes of another. Ask your significant other, or your teenager, to sit down with you. Watch those eyes. You will notice that those eyes move constantly. You have probably heard that this means that person is "shifty" or "sneaky," they "can't be trusted," or some other vague descriptor people use to explain what they don't understand. The fact is, the eyes are simply searching, searching to attach some corresponding memory to comprehend what is being said or seen. It is in which direction he goes with that eye movement that will be important to you.

When asked a question, the eyes will go to the *recall* area of the brain to retrieve the answer to your question. When he doesn't know, or can't find the truth, or is trying to conceal the truth, he will look to the *"I'm making this stuff up"* portion of the brain to bring you back an answer.

Here is how that works. Imagine your brain to be like the hard drive of a computer; your eyes like the screen on your monitor. Your hard drive has many files, and so does your brain. The screen, of course, is where the images are brought to be seen. When you want to recall a memory… something you saw, something you heard, a place you visited, or even when you just want to *go inside* to have a conversation with yourself, you will involuntarily, and (pardon the pun) in the flash of an eye, "send" your eyes to that portion of the brain where those memories are stored. The eyes will *see* that memory, "pick it up," and bring it back to your screen. The screen in this case meaning that when your eyes have finished their search, they will return to center again. That which was recalled or imagined (made up) is now available to be verbalized. If you are watching carefully, you will be able to tell if the answer shared out loud was an actual memory, or just a story that was "made-up."

To better understand where our mental images are stored… where we recall the truth or where we imagined it… note the following illustration. On that drawing you'll notice lines drawn across the plane of the face. These lines reveal the three zones or general areas of your "hard drive" where your memories and metal images are stored: the visual above, the auditory across, and the kinesthetic below.

The Eyes have it!

Drawn for Right Handed preference   (Reverse for Left Handed people)

Visual Recall — **Visual** Construct

Audio Recall — Audio Construct

Kinesthetic (Feeling) Recall — Self Talk

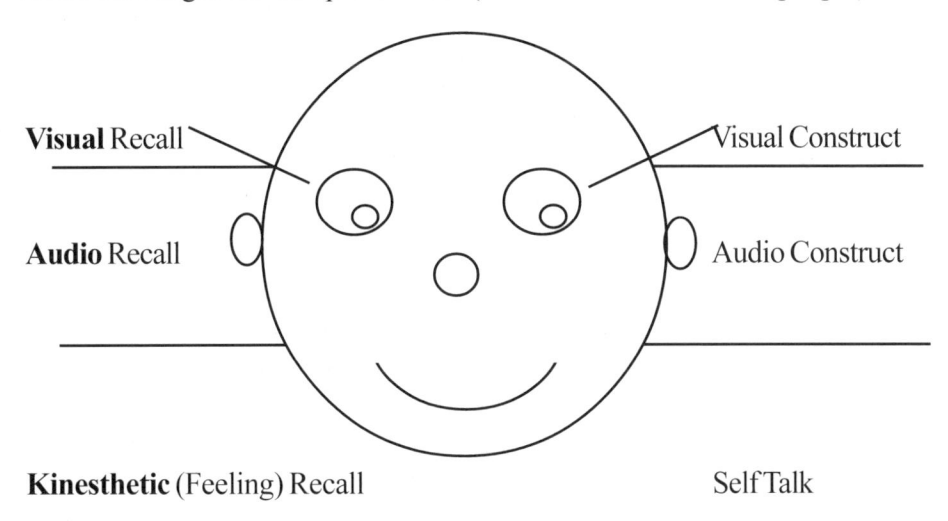

Illustration: "INSTANT RAPPORT" by Michael Brooks

When accessing information, your eyes will automatically search the "hard drive" of your mind to recover the information from one of those zones and return it to the *"screen."* Where that information is *stored* or *constructed* will help you determine the difference between what is REAL from what has been IMAGINED. When a person accesses an actual experience, a visual or auditory memory exists. When asked to recall that memory, the eyes will search for the information and must "see" it to bring it back. If it has not been experienced, there can be no actual corresponding memory to recall. If the experience is NOT there… there is nothing to bring back. If the person knows the truth, but hopes to keep the truth concealed, he/she will search the construct side to *create a response*, bring it back to the screen (to you) and hope you didn't figure out it was a "made-up" answer.

An Aside: When my son was a teenager, I once walked past the family room in our house and heard him on the phone. What caught my attention was this: *"I can't… I tell you I can't! No, I can't lie to my dad. I've tried. No, I don't know how he does it. I think he reads minds!"*

When seeking a <u>visual</u> image, the eyes will *go up* to find it. When seeking an <u>auditory</u> cue, perhaps a song, a poem, a conversation, etc., the eyes will move *laterally*. Generally speaking, you will look to your RIGHT side to RECALL a memory if you are a right handed person. You will look to the LEFT side to RECALL if you are a left handed person. When sitting with your child or significant others, the only way to know for sure is to start by asking questions and seeking responses for which you already know the answers. (More information on this in Chapter 12)

If the person is having a <u>kinesthetic</u> experience, that is, when he is mentally reliving something "hands-on," the eyes will go down and to the side. When people are having a conversation with themselves, the most important person in their lives…the eyes will go down and to the *other* side. Have you ever noticed that when you feel the urge to cry, but you are trying to avoid it, where do you look? You look UP…as far *away from your feeling* or kinesthetic region as possible.

Silence and Proximity

A spouse might use silence as a weapon, a father can punish a child with a stare, or the child will pout in silence as a well practiced method of control. In the same way we communicate with words, inflection and other forms of body language, we also 'speak' when we are *saying* nothing at all.

The mind is relentless. You don't see a dirty milk truck driving down the street, as this might send the message that the contents within might also be "dirty." Shampoo commercials feature models and movie stars. The silent message is clear, *"Use this product and you too can be as pretty as me."* You open a magazine and see a new car advertisement. Lying across the front of the car is a model in a skimpy outfit silently proclaiming, *"Sex sells."* With everything from what you wear and the food you buy, to the car you drive and the way you carry yourself, in virtually every aspect of daily life, you are saying something about yourself with these silent messages.

We humans are conditioned to expressing ourselves with words. As a result, we are naturally uncomfortable with silence. If you don't believe we allow silence to make us uncomfortable, then step onto an elevator with strangers… or ride in a car with people you don't know very well. When that happened, what were you thinking?

In the absence of communications we can speculate for hours on what is imagined. Consequently, we have come to recognize how silence can be deafening. We wonder what *they* are thinking. *"What do they want? Should I do this… or say that? What should I do with my hands (you know, to conceal my nervousness, my insecurity, to hide what I'm really thinking)? How do I look? Is my hair combed? I just know they are focusing on my zit. They probably think I'm ugly. Did she just look at her watch? Was that a smile or a smirk? Yeah, that was a smile, she liked what I said."*

Wordless messages, in many ways, can be even more powerful than our verbal expressions. In our silence, what is implied… in everything from our attitudes to our yearnings… is left up to the imagination of others to interpret. And the human mind, we already know, will speculate for hours about what it does not understand, filling the void with what is imagined. The silent, yet visible reactions received from those "getting the message" allow us to see if our message was received. Without having to commit ourselves, as we do with words and inflection, the reaction we receive from our silent messages allows for "a way out" if our message was misinterpreted or not accepted as we might have anticipated. For as long as I don't say it out loud, I can always say, *"No, that may be what you thought, but that is not what I meant."* On and on the mind races in endless attempts to *explain* what has been *imagined* in silence.

Attorneys, police, salesmen and reporters are among professional groups who are taught the importance of silence. A salesman, for example, is taught that following the sales pitch, the next one to speak "loses." For in that impregnated silence, the moment right after the pitch, the salesman knows that statistically this is when he will experience the highest percentage of his sales. Every time he speaks after the pitch, the odds on the customer buying his product statistically diminish.

A reporter knows he will get the one being interviewed to speak beyond a yes or no response if he/she *uses* the silence. By asking a question and *waiting* beyond the anticipated response, the one being interviewed will invariably say more. He will continue to speak to end the uncomfortable silence. A famous baseball player was asked if he bet on baseball games. After his initial response of "No," the microphone remained extended in front of the player with dead silence for a full three seconds…just enough time to allow the player to incriminate himself. The player blurted: *"Well, it was only $50,000 on one game."*

When it comes to speaking before a group, many would say only that they are afraid to speak before an audience. In truth, it is not our fear of *speaking* we must overcome; it is the fear of SILENCE. Every teacher, politician or other professional, before being turned loose on classrooms, customers, or constituents, first took a Dale Carnegie course or that most basic, "Speech 101" class. In your case, you may have taken a formal Interpersonal Communications course, that speech class most first year college students dread.

In that class you may have found it odd to learn that silence, not sound, was your enemy. Think back over your experiences and those teachers and presenters you endured. How many struck you as not being prepared, or who were more concerned with their agenda than your understanding, or who "forgot" their lines by hoping to memorize rather than familiarize themselves with their text? Listen to an interview or to your politicians as they mentally search for just the right words to continue. In each example, rather than injecting a natural pause, the inexperienced, impromptu or self-absorbed speaker would undoubtedly seek to *fill* the uncomfortable silence with sound; meaningless sound. These are referred to as non-words or "fillers." Ever hear these before? *"Uh; And uh; Ummm, I'm uh, Well uh, Ya know?"*

Actually, as I am typing this I am half listening to CNN in the background. At this moment, I just heard one of our representatives respond to a question with this answer: "Well, now Bob, you know…you know how it is. I am, *ummm...uhh*, I am, uhh, going to, *uhh,* going to, *uhh* vote for this, *uhh,* this bill in the house next week." How many presenters have you been subjected to that speak… but say nothing at all? They would choose instead to fill the air with mere sounds rather than substance?

> **An Aside:** "Ya know?" In the absence of descriptive language to express themselves, many will keep injecting "Ya know?" into each sentence. What they are saying to you is: "*I desperately want you to see the same (mental) pictures I am seeing, ya know? But I don't know how to describe it, ya know, ya know what I mean?"* Never being sure you understand, the speaker is searching for understanding; watching and waiting for you to nod, to say *"OK, I SEE it, too!"*

Proximity

Other intangible, non-spoken, silent messages come out of our subconscious (and conscious) responses to touch and proximity. For example, step up to someone you don't know very well. If you place yourself within 18" of that individual, you will notice him/her physically pulling back. This 0 – 18" is referred to as your *Intimacy Space*. No one enters your intimacy space without your permission. You protect this space and express how uncomfortable it makes you feel when it is violated. Within your intimacy space is hugging… and even in this we send different messages. Hugging side to side conveys equity and friendship; embracing from behind suggests unity and might be best reserved for spouses; an arms open, full frontal hug says complete openness…nothing to hide.

The space extending from 18" to 4' is referred to as your *Personal Space.* This is the area where your intention is to keep people "at arm's length." You gauge this space to determine where friends and social acquaintances will fall. If you pulled up a chair at a diner or the library, and there were three other seats at your table, you would put your books on one side, your umbrella and coat on the other side and if someone comes to sit with you, *you* determine where they will sit. If they are to be kept at "arm's length," the chair across from you is open. If they are close companions, you can invite them beside you and move your items. These are decisions you are making as nonverbal statements to others. You will notice more and more, diners and coffee house tables are round, not square. Studies reveal that people are more comfortable sitting by themselves at a round table.

Your *Social Space* extends to up to 12 feet. Salesmen are taught the importance of this. When the vacuum salesman is invited into your home, he (she) sits on a piece of furniture parallel to the chair or couch you are sitting on. In doing this, he is in your Social Space, but still respecting your Personal Space. After the social amenities, and after he has explained some of the features of his vacuum, he will hold an item, the contract perhaps, and say something like, *"Can I sit there (closer to you) and show you this?"* You, of course, are now on a first name basis so you say, *"Sure."* He has now moved, with your permission, from your *Social* Space, into your *Personal* Space.

A Final Thought:

Remember what the little girl said in *Clan of the Cave Bear*: *"Because they could not speak, they could not lie."* While we are conditioned only to hear… and not to *look* for our communication cues, we consciously miss as much as 80% of the messages that are sent. The best part is, you can practice reading body messages any time you want. Try this: Tonight, when you turn on your television, tune into any reality show or sitcom. For the first 15 minutes turn the sound down and read only what you *observe*. In this way, you can also practice lip reading. In the next 15 minutes, turn the sound up so you can match what you saw with what you are hearing. Other than a punch line or two, there is a very good chance you didn't miss much. This is an excellent process to sharpen your powers of observation.

Chapter 12

Putting it all Together: Passive to Active Listening... in 21 Days...Guaranteed!

*"It takes two to speak the truth —
one to speak and another to listen."*
—Henry David Thoreau

If you were a student or a science teacher in the late sixties and seventies, you certainly remember a popular 16 mm film used in every Life Science or Biology class ever taught. The movie was called "HEMO the Magnificent." It was the story of blood (hemoglobin). It was active, educational, entertaining, and it kept the children mesmerized. It took two class periods to see it all.

After showing the first part of the movie on day one, I was preparing part II for viewing when the students walked back into class the following day. As soon as she crossed the threshold, one little girl couldn't wait to tell me what she thought about it. *"Oh, Mr. Faller,"* she blurted, *"that movie was so good; it really kept my attention. I was so excited! Are we going to see the second part of that movie today? I told my parents all about it. Are we going to see part II about "HOMO, the Magnificent?"*

What? She told her parents *what*?

What follows are tangible, proven strategies to improve your relationships with your students, your family, your faculty, your parents, or anyone. You already know of at least one person with whom you want a better rapport. You may already have that person in mind. You want to see *him* (or her) change, to see *him* become more positive, more open, and more friendly to you. You are secretly hoping that he will read this book because *he* needs it. You wish that somehow you could magically just "fix" him, get *him* to change, to see things the way you do. The problem with that is, those you wish you could *fix*... don't see themselves as broken.

The fact is, the only person you have any control over is you. You can only *FIX*... you. You want others to change... and they will; but they will not change, they *cannot* change, until *they* first recognize a change in the most important person in *your* life... YOU.

It's time to pull all this together. Ready? I'm going to ask you to accept the 21 day challenge. In educational jargon, these are your Objectives and your Action Steps. We're going to do this in three parts.

- Part I: For our first Objective I am going to ask you to choose someone with whom you want to have a better relationship. I will be asking you only to offer simple, basic, sincere affirmation to this person… for 21 days.
- In Part II we pull together our understanding of Words, Inflection and Body Language by applying the four "A's" of Active Listening.
- Part III is going to ask you to take these four "A's" and use them to sharpen your listening skills, build rapport, establish desired relationships, diminish Intrapersonal confusion and resolve your Interpersonal conflicts.

The Basics:

First, think of that person with whom you want to have a better relationship. Take a minute, this is important. Is it your son or daughter, your husband or wife, a troubled student, an angry parent, an uncooperative co-worker? Keep that person foremost in your mind as we move through each of these next three parts. Check your calendar. On the day you choose to begin, count off 21 days on that calendar and put a star on that date. If you want others to treat you differently, more positively, to do it willingly, to do it with a smile… and they won't even realize why they're doing it… you will be amazed how this can happen in just 21 days (or less).

During these 21 days, focus your attention, these strategies, on this one person with whom you want a better rapport. Yes, this will work on other people in your life as well, but it is important that you concentrate on only *one* person right now. This will allow you time to practice, to become comfortable with these simple strategies, and to recognize the subtle changes, (in others and yourself) that will silently confirm that you are on the right track. Focusing on just one person for now will allow you to observe the changes (in you and him/her) as they happen.

Not to belabor this much further, but please note: Many will see the steps below as simple, easy to follow, common-sense approaches to diminishing conflict and establishing better relationships with others. Consequently, they will want to try this on everyone at once. As a result, they will become overwhelmed, frustrated, distracted, give up and revert back into old, unproductive habits, and wonder why. My best advice is, trust the process. Be patient, become comfortable with the simple strategies by placing your attention on this one person for now.

You know you want a better relationship with this individual you've chosen, but you are not going to have a better relationship with anyone if you just *hope* for it. You are soon going to be 21 days older anyway, whether you tried what I'm offering you or not. So what do you have to lose? It will cost you nothing. You are going to see that person everyday anyway. You said you wanted a better rapport with this person, so you have everything to gain, and nothing to lose. You will be amazed at the results…I guarantee it.

Fact: What you are about to enter into will take some focused effort. I suggest that you follow this process to the extent you are comfortable doing so.

1. *First choose **ONE** individual with whom you want to have a better relationship.* Yes, it will work with virtually everyone but just focus on ONE for now while you are developing the habits that will work on everyone. You will find it easier to build these habits and to see that it really works if you focus on just ONE for now. Note: if you pick a student or coworker, your 21 days will be 21 school or work days; if you choose a family member, someone you see daily, it will be 21 *consecutive* days.

2. You are also going to need a practice partner to work with so you can support and encourage each other. You are looking for a close friend or colleague; hopefully someone who will be accepting this 21 day challenge, too. You will need someone to bounce ideas off; someone to "practice with." Seminar participants often 'buddy-up' before they leave the session. The idea is to choose someone who also wants to learn more, as you do.

3. Now find a calendar to mark your next 21 days. Yes, a real calendar so you will have a tangible way to both measure your progress and to remember to follow through on what you are about to do for all 21 days. Remind your supportive partner, as she/he will remind you, to mark it daily.

4. Next (this is optional); secure a notebook…put it with your calendar. Use it like a diary for 21 days to log your observations, comments, responses, thoughts, feelings, etc., regarding your efforts to improve this relationship. When you read back over this, you will *see* how, step by step, you have been forming a relationship built on meeting the Needs of another. Without the log, you may not appreciate that every journey is measured in increments.

Part I

The 21 Day Challenge:
Meeting the Need to be Affirmed and Accepted

WE BEGIN:

First allow me to avoid constantly writing him or her…or herself or himself…she or he, all the way through this. Please allow my use of interchangeable pronouns…as you have noticed throughout this book…to be inclusive of both genders.

> Ready? On day one, and every day during this challenge, find something positive to affirm him with. That's it! But be sincere. Don't "make it up." If you are phony… people will read through you. Neither does it have to be elaborate. The operative word here is SINCERE, as in *sincere*, simple, basic, and honest affirmation… *everyday.*

A few years ago, I was counseling a man and his wife. I spoke with them together, then separately. I suggested to the wife that she try this 21 day challenge to provide some affirmation to her husband, to do it everyday… for 21 days. She understood the goal was to become more positive and affirming, and she was willing to do this as a strategy to building new and more positive habits in her life. After seven days she came back to the office and said, *"I can't do it anymore! I can't find anything else nice to say about him!"*

If *you* are not willing to try to promote a better relationship, to find something *nice to say about him,* then this exercise won't last 21 days with you, either. Remember, I keep saying "21 days" because it takes 21 days to develop a new habit. AFTER 21 days, it will become second nature to you. You will find your affirmations, your *nice things to say*, to come more freely and naturally. If it doesn't flow naturally from you already… it will. Your motivation to continue will be the returned affirmation and satisfaction that awaits you.

Remember your notebook: You'll want to log in your "diary" everyday for those 21 days. These will be *your observations* of the experience. DO NOT be discouraged if he does NOT affirm you back! In fact, for several days, don't be surprised if you are basically ignored after you offer your affirmation. The Need to be Accepted and the Need to be Affirmed are powerful human Needs that ALL of us have. Whether or not the person you have been affirming acknowledges your comments or not… know that she *heard* you and loved the attention.

Your affirmation WILL have an impact. Others will, slowly at first, show signs that your affirmations are being returned to you. As you go back over your 'diary' from day one, you'll see it for yourself how your affirmations elicited more positive behaviors: the "looks," the quiet smiles, the greetings, the surprise visit *"just to say hello,"* are all examples that demonstrate that you are breaking through. That's why you're keeping the log… to reflect over the previous few weeks to see *how it happened.*

I remember counseling a mom and her teenager. We spoke together and then we spoke separately. The teenager was 'suffering' from a typical case of "All About Me." The mother thought she was "losing her baby," which she was, because her baby grew into a teenager and mom missed it. The teen, of course, wanted to know that she was loved by pretending she hated her parents and all that they stood for. (Just work with it, somehow it makes perfect sense to a teenager.)

I asked the mother to affirm her daughter, sincerely, openly, honestly and without expectations in return… for 21 days. The mother did so. In typical fashion, the mother reported that during the first few days, she received such comebacks as *"What's wrong?"* and *"What did I do THIS time?"* Mother was prepared for this so she dutifully ignored the barbs and continued to drop well placed affirmations on her daughter every day. I also warned mom about the "silence period" that might happen over the following couple of weeks. In fact, mother reported that the daughter not only didn't acknowledge her, she actually withdrew, pouted, and ignored her. Mom understood that the child *heard* her affirmations even if the daughter refused eye contact when she "got it." Mom knew this was the daughter's "testing period" to see if mom's affirmations were sincere. Applying the Rule of Opposites (book 2, *"So THAT's why you're like that!"*) the teen is exhibiting opposite behaviors to get what she wants. She is silently pleading…with what an adult would view as illogical behaviors…for the positive attention to continue.

Nearing the end of the third week, as the mother noted in the log she had been keeping, she could none-the-less, see subtle, but positive responses coming from her daughter. Her bedroom was, as mom wrote, *"gradually beginning to take shape."* She came *"out of her room to play a board game Thursday night."* But the day that got mom choked up was the day she knew that positive affirmations…*without expecting it in return…*could bring people closer together. She wrote that her daughter went to her bedroom after dinner (as usual) but returned a few minutes later and asked, *"Mom, can I help you with the dishes?"* Mom's quote in the diary said it all, *"I almost passed out! I gave her a hug and saw her smile again. My daughter was coming back to me!"*

Try it for yourself for 21 days. What do you have to *gain*?

PART II

The FOUR "A's" of Active Listening
The Heart of Active Listening

Attitude
Acknowledge
Aim the Posture
AYE *(Eye) Contact

*(*Ok, so I was kidding about AYE for EYE contact. But really, isn't 4 "A's" much easier to remember than 3 "A's" and an E?*)

It is time to exercise another strategy for building positive relationships: Active Listening. Remember, as with the directed affirmation suggested in Part 1, you are not expected to do this with everyone you meet... yet. I recommend that you first focus on...practice on...only ONE person. You can select the same person, or perhaps you already have another person in mind. These 4 "A's" are the basics, easy to remember and are the essential elements that must be applied to every conversation you are about to have with the person you selected... for another 21 days. Become comfortable with the four A's, then move to Part 3.

ATTITUDE:
"This is OUR conversation, not yours or mine, it is our conversation... but I will NOT steal the focus."

A guaranteed 'deal breaker' in your attempts to build positive, lasting relationships is when one person in the dynamic receives the message: "*You are not important to me.*" That may not be the intent, but each time the focus is stolen from the speaker, this is clearly the message being received. You know that we all associate what we hear with our own experiences. This association is, after all, our common-union of understanding; the very definition of communications.

To hear what another says and to flash to an associated memory is perfectly natural. The speaker tells you about her trip to the mall, and you immediately see a related experience YOU had at the mall. If she tells you about her grandchild, you immediately envision a similar experience YOU had with your grandchild. To react to the urge to interrupt the speaker, to inject your thoughts or to seek an opening so that you can insert your own agenda...is *not* natural. Yes, many do just that, but the *Attitude* of an Active Listener must be; "*This conversation is NOT about me. I will NOT steal the focus from the speaker.*"

If you have the ATTITUDE that this is *our* conversation but *your* agenda, the next thing your speaker will want to know is… *"Did you hear me?"*

ACKNOWLEDGE:
Let the speaker SEE that he/she has been heard.

It is a rare day when we actually find people who have the ATTITUDE to do what is being asked: *"Listen to me."* It is not easy to put your own agenda aside to completely listen to another. If you have the ATTITUDE, then ACKNOWLEDGING that you understand what you are hearing is the perfect validation to confirm, "I'm LISTENING!"

When *you* speak with another, you want to know that you have been heard. Others want to know that they are being heard, too. It is essential for the speaker to believe that what she (he) is saying is being "taken in" by the listener. Just like a cash register rings every time it opens, the listener nods the head, uses inflection and offers comments to provide the immediate feedback the speaker requires each time she "makes a deposit."

There are a number of ways to say, *"Yes, I'm with you!"*

You can acknowledge with a single word: *"Yes...Really? Fascinating... Wonderful! Unbelievable.*

You can repeat back: *"Did you just say 27? How often? Were you alone?"*

You can respond with new knowledge: *"I had no idea… I could never get that to work for me… I can't wait to try that myself… That is amazing…"*

You can question: *"Do you think that would work for me? What step should I take first? How does this happen? So, where was it hidden?"*

You can model: We know that words cannot convey intent; the meaning of words can be entirely too subjective to rely on them for understanding. Yet most of us do just that; we rely on the face value of words alone for our understanding. You can continue to understand at this level, or you can go deeper, looking beyond the simple meaning of words to *enter the speaker's* Visual, Auditory or Kinesthetic *World of Understanding* by modeling their pattern of speech.

Anytime you say you want to have a relationship with someone, you are saying that you want to *relate* to that person. How easy is it to relate to someone who speaks in a foreign language? Your chances of establishing a relationship would be greatly improved if you spoke in a language he is familiar with and accustomed to using. Language is, after all, the framework that connects us, bringing us together into a common *world of understanding*. We relate to those who *"speak our language."*

To enter the world of another, to *"speak his language,"* use the language expressed in the speaker's a*ction* verbs. Listen as he speaks. Focus intently on his *action* words as he tells you a story. The action verbs he *predominately* uses will describe his learning modality. His preferred modality is what he is using to describe the pictures in his head. To relate to him, speak to him in his own language…out of

HIS world of understanding…in even the same words if you want him to accept you as someone who *"really understands me."* He is speaking in a language he understands: visual, auditory, or kinesthetic. Why would you respond to him in a foreign language?

Examples of **Visual** cues:
See, Observe, Spy, View, Witness, Spot, Look, Glimpse, Peer, Peek, Examine, Inspect, Stare, Glare, Show

Examples of **Auditory** cues:
Listen, Hear, Overhear, Sound, Ring, Chime, Scream, Speak, Whisper, Talk, Buzz, Call, Click, Ring my bell

Examples of **Kinesthetic** cues:
Bite, Burst, Bind, Break, Fall, Fight, Catch, Grasp, Grab, Hit, Hold, Climb, Run, Struggle, Throw, Toss, Walk, Jump

While none of us are visual, auditory *or* kinesthetic, we do hold a preference for one modality over the others. This is how we learn best. We best relate to others who are like us. We *like* people who are like us…or who we want to be like. We tend not to like or not to trust people who are *not* like us. If you have an auditory preference, for example, you are LESS apt to hear and accept my instructions or advice if I am speaking out of a world of understanding *foreign* to that of your own. Knowing that, I would attempt to relate to you by conversing with the auditory language you were most comfortable with.

Even though you have been reading this text instead of listening to me express it, have you noticed what *Action Verbs* I have been using? Listen to the action words in my sentences…anyone's sentences…and you can hear the preference toward being visual, auditory or kinesthetic. If you are willing to focus on the speaker's *action,* he will freely offer you the style of learning that best suits him. He will be giving you the keys that will unlock the pathway to his *world of understanding.* You do this because you want to *relate* to him. You will RELATE to people who RELATE to you. Others will relate to YOU…if you make an effort to relate to THEM.

Let's say your speaker is a VISUAL person. As a visual person, his ACTION verbs might *look* something like this:

"I don't **SEE** any way out of this. Someone is always **WATCHING** me. It's as if someone is always **LOOKING** over my shoulder, **GLARING** at me whenever I make a mistake."

He is speaking out of his *world of understanding,* so you would not want to respond in a "foreign language" with action verbs out of a different world of understanding. You would not, for example, want to *jump* back with a KINESTHETIC or AUDITORY response like this:

"It **SOUNDS** like this happens often? Yes, I **CATCH** your point; you've been **FIGHTING** this **STRUGGLE** for some time now.

You will, instead, want to "speak his language" and acknowledge this VISUAL person with similar language, with "sight" words out of his own world of understanding:
*"I **SEE**; it **APPEARS** like you've been **WATCHING** this for a long time now. It **LOOKS** like you're having trouble **SEEING** your way out of this."*

AIM YOUR POSTURE:
"If you won't face me, how can I believe you care about me?"

From the foundation of the earliest Christian church, the wedding ceremony has included this question: *"Do you promise to love, honor and obey?"* The love and honor part sounded good, but many a prospective spouse has held reservations about committing to that word, OBEY. When she heard her minister ask this question, one bride who froze at the altar told me she did so because of that word: Obey. She said, *"In that moment I knew I didn't want to marry him to be his servant."* She saw Obey to mean: "be subservient to your husband."

Words do hold powerful images for us. What if the original meaning of the word, the one that has been used in wedding vows for centuries, was not saying, *"do as you're told,"* but was intended instead as a vow between couples to *maintain harmony*. The literal definition of Obey, which has gotten lost in our modern "all about me" world, asked the prospective bride and groom to *"place yourself in a position to listen"* during times of misunderstandings and strife. True communications and conflict resolution are dependent upon two (or more) people being willing to be open; to put themselves in a *position to listen* to the other. The intent seems clear: be *equal* to one another, as opposed to the more modern perspective, be *subordinate* to another. Conflict can be diminished with such a vow to LISTEN to one another.

When I present this seminar on Active Listening, I sometimes will ask two people to literally put themselves *in a position to listen*. I will ask them to sit facing each other on stage to conduct an experiment. The intent, of course, is to demonstrate the incredible importance of body language and how "AIMING" your body conveys the listener's intent to be open and "in a position" to listen. I ask one of my volunteers on stage to be the speaker and to share a story with the listener. The listener is to be practicing these Four "A's" of Active Listening as the speaker tells her story.

While the two individuals are engaged in conversation, I am off to one side of the stage where only the "listener" in this demonstration could see me. When the speaker "gets into" her story, I nod to the listener. By prearrangement, the listener shifts his chair and body ¼ turn from the speaker, but in all other ways, continues to offer attention to the speaker. A few moments later, still with a straight face, the listener sees the signal and will turn another ¼ turn; now with his back to the speaker.

The NEED to be Affirmed (to be heard) is powerful. Even as the listener turns the first ¼ turn, the speaker might pause, but will invariably continue with her story. The speaker will, often involuntarily but noticeably, shift her position to follow the turn…stretching the torso, the head, leaning forward in the seat…in an attempt to again re-AIM her posture…and reconnect with her listener.

When the listener makes the full 180 degree turn, I have seen speakers that are now so *into* their story, that without missing a beat, they would physically stand up, pick up their own chair and walk around to the front of the listener to continue as if nothing happened. Facing your listener/speaker is THAT important. Most people in such demonstrations, however, will just give up, immediately reading the "listener's" body language as saying, *"I really don't care."* Your body language, how you "AIM" *your* body, sends the message that *"I care"* much louder than any words you could speak.

Speakers must believe that you care about them; about what they have to say. Facing the speaker… Aiming your Posture…is essential in conveying your sincerity. You can't always determine when a conversation will take place. You might be at a table with the speaker across from you where "aiming" is easy; or side by side in auditorium seats where aiming your body is difficult; or riding in a car where full body frontage is impossible. Wherever you find this conversation unfolding, simply ask yourself, *"How can I place myself (AIM my posture) to be in the best position to listen?"*

When determining how much to give when Aiming your Posture, allow this to be your rule of thumb: *give what you get.* If, for example, the person standing beside you is facing you while you are facing away; TURN…and better Aim your body. If your speaker can't turn but a ¼ turn to face you, give back the same positioning. (If he is driving and turns his head…tell him to pull over and YOU drive.)

EYE *("Aye")* CONTACT
The eyes are referred to as the "gateway to the soul."

The eyes are referred to as the most valued Interpersonal communication asset you possess (Chapter 11). Here is your assignment: practice with your partner to observe eye movement. Detect how the eyes process thought and how they respond to questions. Your 'practice' partner will allow you to ask questions, provide observations and to 'make mistakes' as you support each other in fostering these Interpersonal skills. With your practice partner:

~Watch his eyes as they respond to your questions. Become comfortable when the eyes "search" for the answer. Right handed persons will GENERALLY seek recall on THEIR right side…Left handed people will be just the opposite. That is why I would suggest that you first ask pointed questions for which you already know the answers so you can determine the RECALL side from the CONSTRUCT side.

~Watch those eyes look up and to the left or right when you ask her VISUAL RECALL questions, i.e., *How many traffic lights between here and your home? How many windows are in your house? How many different colored carpets are in your house? How many boys are in your class?* The eyes will flash to SEE that information, and bring it back to the "screen." You will know when she "found" the answer as those eyes are now looking at you again. You will also be comfortable identifying which side is the RECALL side if you start off asking questions for which you already know the answer. For example, ask her *"What did you have for lunch today?"* Ask her to tell you the truth…then ask her to make-up an answer. What do you notice?

~VISUAL CONSTRUCT (the answer is being "made-up") questions will take the speaker's eyes up and to the *opposite* side of Visual Recall. Watch those eyes when you ask such questions as: *"Imagine yourself with purple hair* (unless of course, she has or had purple hair…then she will RECALL it). If you know she has never been on a cruise, ask her, *"What was your favorite part of taking a cruise?"* She will 'search' for a memory that isn't there…so she will have to construct, or make-up an answer. To which side did she look for that?

~In the same way, ask her to demonstrate AUDITORY RECALL. She will look laterally toward the ear. Ask something you know the answer to. Ask her to recite the preamble to the constitution, or to sing the birthday song. (She won't have to say it out loud, just watch the eyes for your answer. Ask her, *"What did Mary really tell you last night?"* or *"What were the last words you heard when you left the house this morning?"* If she is CONSTRUCTING an answer she will look to the *opposite* side.

Practice by asking questions of your training partner; questions for which you KNOW the answers. Watch and recognize where the eyes go to "search" for your answer. This is why it is best to practice with a partner. Ask your partner if you are guessing correctly until you are able to tell him what you believe he is "saying" with his eyes. Your partner can validate your observations and will tell you if he "made it up" or if he brought back the truth. The more you practice… like anything else… the more comfortable you will become in its use.

Here are some other things to practice:

~Practice on being more attentive to your speaker, rather than thinking, *"What will I say next?"* As a way to practice on focusing, see if you can determine if this person has a preference toward the Visual, the Auditory or the Kinesthetic by listening intently to your speaker's *action verbs*. (review Action Verbs section in Chapter 9)

~Listen to the inflection: what is being said… and what *isn't* being said by the absence of inflection. (Chapter 10)

~Practice PACING the speaker's body with your body; matching her body language with your own. (Chapter 11) Let her see HER reflection… in YOU. After PACING for a while, try *breaking* the pace to see if rapport has been established. This is referred to as MIRRORING. When you casually cross your legs or arms, or shift in your seat, see if the one you are listening to… the one you are hoping to rapport with… is now pacing YOU.

PART III
Putting it into Practice

If you have read, understood and practiced the 4 "A's," you are prepared to actively listen to the person you selected. Follow the four "A's" each time you have the opportunity over the next 21 days. As they say in the commercials… "Just DO IT."

EVERYTIME you have an opportunity to have a conversation with the person you select, be it a one sentence meeting or a 10 minute chat… listen to that person. Listen completely, empathetically and sincerely. In other words, this means focus on those 4 "A's." This doesn't have to be "perfect" each time. There will be no written test so try to own these "A's" rather than trying to memorize them; be comfortable, be patient, be at peace with the process.

> **A**… Attitude: OUR conversation… but YOUR agenda. Focus on the speaker.
> **A**… Acknowledge what you heard (make it natural… not exaggerated).
> **A**… Aim your body: "Giving what you get." It shows you are being attentive to the speaker. Allow the speaker to recognize, *"YES, you really are listening."*
> **A**…(Aye) Eye contact is critical: provide eye contact… without staring.

Most of us have been conditioned to watching the world with *the sound up*. We do not observe, we count primarily on our hearing for understanding. Until we choose to step out of what has been comfortable and easy, to form new habits, to become a more active, empathetic and complete listener, we will be choosing to remain in a very limited world of understanding. I encourage you to begin today; to begin NOW.

A Final Thought:

You have always wanted others to treat you differently, more positively. You have hoped for it, but how have you worked for it? You have exercised endless methods of control to convince people to pay attention to *you* – to like *you*. Both consciously and subconsciously you have been seeking out ways to gain the acceptance of others. It can be exhausting, can't it?

If you have decided to become a more effective listener, picking up on what others are saying with their words, inflection and body language, you have chosen to become a more effective communicator. You have everything to gain, virtually nothing to lose. In doing so, you will be amazed to discover that others *will* notice. They won't understand why, nor will they care. They will care only that *you* are now, somehow, for whatever reason, paying more focused attention to *them*. They will notice that you care, that you are giving them better eye contact, and that you are making a sincere effort to truly understand them.

The most phenomenal part is…when you are willing to give up the struggle to prove that life is first and foremost, all about YOU…*you* will discover that what you first offered to others, will now come back to you. With practice, your attentiveness to listening through sound and observation *will* become effortless. You will no longer be choosing selective behaviors to momentarily garner the attention of others. New and more productive habits will replace controlling behaviors. Without conscious thought, others will begin treating you differently, more positively. They will do it willingly, they will do it for life, and they won't even realize why they're doing it… guaranteed!

Soon, others will be saying to you… ***"I'm LISTENING!"***

Epilogue

Listen * Listen * Listen

In our country we have treatment facilities for emotionally disturbed adolescents. Some are called: Most Intensive. These two words mean that children who reside in such centers, as young as eleven to as old as seventeen, were all court ordered to be there. Each having deep emotional scars and may well have been sexually and/or physically abused. This is a lock-up facility for adolescents. The severe nature of their emotional distress requires that these children be under 24 hour supervision. If these children were to run away from this facility, you know where they would go? Most would run straight back to their homes, to the very people who abused them. What an incredible statement on human nature: our human Needs are stronger than our Fears.

In one such facility, a counselor found this letter left by a teenage girl (spelling and punctuation corrected). In that letter you can hear her despair. Note: Suicide is the leading cause of death among teenagers.

"I know I love my parents and that they love me. But they have spoiled my life because they do not listen. Whenever I tried to talk with them they always said, *'Later, I can't talk now, I'm too busy.'* When they did listen they often said to me, *'That's stupid to feel that way about it, or I know, I went through the same thing myself.'* But I know they hadn't gone through the same thing and that they didn't know how I felt at all.

"When they said things like that, or would not listen, then I stopped trying to talk with them at all. It made me feel there was no point in talking to them, and it hurt so much when they misunderstood me or would not pay attention. I guess that is why we didn't get along. I had to act out how I was feeling because they would not listen, but they didn't understand that either and it only made it worse.

"My parents showed their love for me by being responsible. They didn't want me to do anything wrong because this would show they had done something wrong and then God would punish us all. So they sent me to a religious boarding school, they made me go so I wouldn't turn out wrong. They always tried to keep me from doing what was wrong instead of listening to me so I would figure things out for myself.

"So where am I now? I drank too much, took drugs, had lots of sex with boys but no love. I am terribly confused. *The worst thing is that if my parents read this letter they would have no idea who wrote it.* That is why if I had one thing to say to parents (or teachers), it would be stop talking for a while and LISTEN, LISTEN, LISTEN!"

Please do not define love for your child as *keeping her (him) happy.* You might interpret love as what YOU do <u>for</u> your child; but your child may be interpreting LOVE as what you *allow* her to do for herself. When you deny your child the freedom to make her own creative and responsible decisions for herself, you deny for her, the very same freedom you demand for yourself. When you prevent her from accepting consequences for her behaviors, *you* might see this as a sign of your love for your child, but will your *child* see this as love…or only as another rescue from consequence? Keep in mind that children not only want structure in their lives, they will demand it; and they will *act out* until they get it.

No matter how many times you say to your teen, *"I love you,"* he or she cannot possibly get enough. Your child, in the home or at school, will never get his or her fill of these two phrases: *"I love you"* and *"I'm proud of you."* No, you may not always love your child's *behaviors*, but leave no doubt that you still love *the child*. When in doubt as to what to say…repeat the above…and often. Then just LISTEN.

Listening really IS…LOVE in action.

I wish you Peace,

Motivational speaker, Tod Faller

Tod Faller has a Pastoral Ministry Certification in Counseling, an MA degree in Educational Leadership and post graduate doctoral work in Organizational Leadership, Personal Relations and Family Counseling. He has served the profession of education, in both public and private school systems… in Elementary, Secondary and Higher Education… as a teacher, counselor, principal, program director, and independent consultant for more than 35 years. Tod has traveled extensively… literally from Green Bay to Tampa Bay… presenting interactive communication, motivation, and leadership seminars.

Trained in Neuro Linguistic Programming (NLP), Reality Therapy, and Choice Theory, Tod has also provided university graduate instruction in such areas as Adult Development, Work Behavior, Conflict Resolution, Interpersonal Communications, and Motivation Theory.

"People will begin treating YOU differently, more positively, and THEY won't even know why they're doing it… Guaranteed!"

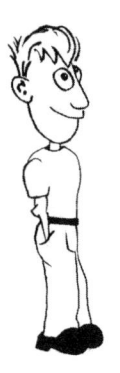

Visit our web site at www.todfaller.com

What People Say about Tod Faller:

"I was totally entertained and captivated from start to finish."
—Lewis County Schools, Keynote Address

"I couldn't believe the high level of enthusiasm maintained through the entire day!" —Boone County, Public Schools

"I've never been so completely enthralled. What a message!"
—Keynote Address

"A comedian with a message." —Martinsburg Public Schools

"A perfect blend of humor with a great message."
—Public Relations Regional Conference

"Wow! What a great story teller. Just… Wow!" —Virginia Alliance

"His seminars are fun, fast paced, interactive and guaranteed to alter the way you look at the people and relationships in your life."
—SREB Annual Conference, Orlando, Fl.

"Outstanding! I can't wait to go back to school to practice what I've learned!"
—Charles City School District, Charles City, Virginia

"I could do this all day! I may never look at others the same way again."
—Tennessee State Middle School Conference

"Awesome! Eye opening. The best training I've ever experienced in 22 years with the state."
—Department of Employment Security

"Excellent! Captivating! Motivating! Great!"
—Broward County Schools, Ft. Lauderdale, Fl.

For more information visit www.TodFaller.com

In the 21st Century, it is still... ALL about the Culture.

"Without a culture FOR Learning, on what shall you build your Communities OF Learning?"

RIGOR is in the content:
RELEVANCE gives significance to the content: but
RELATIONSHIPS drive the content and guarantee delivery.

The Teacher Down the Hall
Books/Audio CD's

"What did you do THAT for?"

"So THAT'S why you're like that!"

I'm Listening

Lessons for Leaders

One-day RELATIONSHIP Building Conference
~The NEGLECTED "R"~
Understanding * Accepting * Resolving Conflict

CONFERENCE OUTLINE

8:15- 8:45 Expectations: Lessons for Learners

8:45- 10:15 Session #1: "What did you do THAT for?"
  Understanding...the Nature of our Human Nature

You can't be expected to understand every human behavior...but you can easily understand the five basic human Needs we all have in common. Learn to look behind the negative or inappropriate behaviors of others to meet the Need that spawned that behavior. Help others to meet their Needs, and they will go out of their way to meet your Needs...Guaranteed!

10:15 – 10:30 Break

10:30 – 12:00 Session #2: "I'm Listening."
  Accepting...the more we're different, the more we're exactly alike.

We all have the basic human Need to be heard but assume that just because we say it, others "get it." True communications and understanding, however, is never in the intent of the speaker; it is always in the message received by the listener. By learning to read and listen to the words, inflection and body language of others, you will be amazed at how others will begin treating you differently, more positively, and they won't even know why they're doing it...GUARANTEED! Relationships will be built and conflicts resolved when you practice these four "A's" of Active Listening.

LUNCH

1:00 – 1:30 Conversations: Leaders and Learners

1:30 – 3:00 Session #3 "Can't we all just get along?"
  Resolving... Interpersonal CONFLICT

Our human BEHAVIORS are what keep us apart; our human NEEDS are what we have in common. But it is our PERSONALITIES that give us balance. In this active, fun and highly charged session, participants will learn their own personality traits, and the traits of those around them. Participants will immediately discover why some people excel in certain tasks, yet flounder in others. And the question will be answered as to why you choose to admire and respect some folks, yet remain in conflict with others.

3:00 -3:30 Revelations: Lessons for Leaders

For more information go to www.TodFaller.com

The "Teacher Down the Hall" Seminar Series

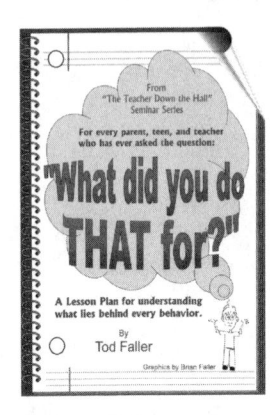

"What did you do THAT for?"—First in the series, this book will help you to look past the behaviors of others to recognize and meet the Needs that motivated those behaviors.
ISBN 0929915372, 7 x 10, 80 pages, paperback, Retail Price $12.95

"So THAT'S why you're like that!" – Second in the seminar series includes more on the nature of our human nature, the application of conflict resolution solutions and the true story of *The Teacher Down the Hall*.
ISBN 0929915372, 80 pages, 7 x 10, paperback, Retail Price $12.95

I'm Listening—Third in the seminar series—highly effective communications is not measured by how much you say...but in how well you listen!
ISBN 0929915704, 7 x 10, 112 pages, paperback, Retail Price $15.95

Lessons for Leaders—Leaders are those who understand human needs, accept human differences, and choose to be a catalyst for conflict resolution solutions—stories, passages and examples from *The Teacher Down the Hall* Seminar Series. ISBN 0929915410, 10 x 7, paperback, 96 pages, $15.95

If you have questions, would like further information, or would like Mr. Faller to speak to your school, business or organization, please contact us at:

Human Resource Leadership Consultants

3005 Brierwood Rd., Culloden, WV 25510
www.todfaller.com
email: tod@todfaller.com

Headline Books, Inc.